What I Wish I Knew
BEFORE
CANCER

by
Nicholas Steven Parscale

Solution Tree | Press

a division of

Solution Tree

555 North Morton Street
Bloomington, IN 47404
800.733.6786 (toll free) / 812.336.7700
FAX: 812.336.7790

email: info@SolutionTree.com
SolutionTree.com

Printed in the United States of America

Solution Tree
Jeffrey C. Jones, CEO
Edmund M. Ackerman, President

Solution Tree Press
President and Publisher: Douglas M. Rife
Associate Publisher: Sarah Payne-Mills
Art Director: Rian Anderson
Managing Production Editor: Kendra Slayton
Copy Chief: Jessi Finn
Content Development Specialist: Amy Rubenstein
Proofreader: Sarah Ludwig
Text and Cover Designer: Rian Anderson
Editorial Assistants: Sarah Ludwig and Elijah Oates

For Mrs. Smith and Greg

Praise for *What I Wish I Knew Before Cancer*

"Nick reminds us of what we already know but is easily forgotten. *What I Wish I Knew Before Cancer* shares what he is learning about life while battling cancer and what is really important. A few favorite pieces of wisdom are:

- Find time to be with friends and to laugh.
- The hard things give you perspective.
- Surround yourself with positive people and positive thoughts.

"Families facing childhood cancer are thrown into a world of unfamiliarity and unknowns, and Nick is an example of someone who thinks beyond himself to help others. Be inspired!"

—Laura Eicher, Senior Pediatrics Initiative Manager, The American Cancer Society

"Cancer is not a curse. Turn your diagnosis into a superpower. That's the message fourteen-year-old Nicholas Parscale delivers in his inspirational and must-read book. No child should have to go head-to-head with cancer. But Nicholas wants you to know he has your back. He is on a mission to help kids like him win the fight of their lives. Told through the eyes of a brave young soul, *What I Wish I Knew Before Cancer* provides a daily life road map full of tips and tricks for beating cancer from diagnosis to remission."

—Jedd Canty, Founder, Canty Ventures

"What you're holding in your hand right now is a gem. Nicholas's story of grit, determination, and always (I mean ALWAYS) moving forward is something you only see in movies. But he lives it daily—with a smile on his face. Nicholas embodies everything I want to be. He is positive, intelligent, and strong beyond words and inspires anyone around him with his infectious energy and smile. If we all learned just one thing from Nicholas, the world would be a much better place. I recommend you read this book (twice) and enjoy Nicholas's journey. Let it inspire you like it did me. Share this book. Share his message. Nicholas, I'm proud to call you my friend, and I look forward to having you on stage soon."

—Mark Evans, Best-Selling Author, Entrepreneur, and Investor

"Children should never have to worry about battling cancer. As a father of two young girls, I watch my kids play and have fun and have no worries. That is what childhood is all about. Cancer should never be something they have to think about growing up. Unfortunately, we see a lot of kids battling cancer. Nicholas has done an amazing job of fighting this disease. Not only is he brave, but he is an inspiration for everyone. Watching Nick embrace life and have fun has been inspiring to me. He has taken an awful situation and found as many positives in it as he can. I think Nick is someone who everyone can look toward for influence. He never seems to be down, and I truly believe his positive attitude is helping him battle this disease. If you are ever in a bad spot, think of Nicholas, think of how positive he is, and get rid of that negative energy. Nick has shown me that anything is possible and that a positive attitude can really go a long way in making your life better!"

—Bob Fescoe, Host, *Fescoe in the Morning*,
KCSP-AM 610 Sports Radio

"Nicholas is an extraordinary young hero with a story that is truly one of strength, character, and bravery. Life hasn't always been kind, but no matter what happens, he never loses his positivity and always finds a way to spread it to others. He is just one of those people whose presence lights up a room, and I will forever be inspired by Nick's excitement for life. Read this book—it will leave an impact on your world!"

—Monica Glass, Chef

"I've never met a kid as selfless as Nicholas Parscale. Throughout his cancer journey, he has been just as concerned in helping others battling this dreadful disease as he has been with his own fight. How many middle schoolers tell you they plan to be an oncologist someday? Nick is truly special, and this very insightful book is yet another facet of his incredible legacy."

—Brian Hanni, Voice of the Jayhawks,
Director of Broadcasting, University of Kansas

"Nicholas Parscale is an amazing gift from God. His journey is one that would be a struggle for one of any age. Nicholas embraced his cross and then let others share his story. Though this book was written primarily for preteens and teenagers, there are blessings on these pages for young and old alike. There is honesty and innocence in each story that reveals a soul that is close to God. My life has been blessed in my knowing Nicholas, and yours will find blessing in reading his story. May we all embrace in faith the crosses that come our way, and may these lead us to the place where Nicholas has chosen to stay: close to the heart of our God."

—Father Michael Mulvany, Pastor, Corpus Christi
Catholic Church, Lawrence, Kansas

Table of Contents

Chapter 1
Some Birthday Surprise 1

The Monster Shows Up 7

My big party, 2016.

Chapter 2
The Best Medicine of All. 15

Let Me Rewind a Little. 16

How to Stay Positive 17

They Say I'm an Old Soul 22

Me and Mom keeping positive.

Chapter 3
What Is Cancer, Anyway? 27

Me waiting to go into the clinic for chemo, 2017. Check out the mask; we were ahead of the times.

Chapter 4
Going Into Whatever's Up Next 31

Trusting Your Team Helps a Lot 31

The Monkey in My Chair Program. . . . 34

You're Going to Get Poked and Prodded . 35

They Like It When You Eat 37

Chemotherapy 37

About Going Bald 43

Radiation 44

The Feeding Tube 45

Me at the clinic with the chemo going into my chest.

Chapter 5
Take Charge of Pain . 49

Regular Pain 51

Don't Be Scared Before It Even Happens . 51

When You Just Get Tired of It 53

The Hardest Kind of Pain 55

Somedays, I just slept a lot.

Chapter 6
You're Not Alone . . . 63

Friendships and Keeping in Touch Under
the Circumstances 64

Special Friends 69

Going Back to School and It's
All Changed! 70

Learning to Deal With How People
See You. 72

Me and my friends, Carolyn, Hailey, Katelyn, and Braden at the Lawrence Aquatic Center.

Chapter 7
Special Opportunities. 77

The Big Slick. 78

Make-A-Wish® Foundation 81

Super Bowl LIV 85

Me and Chef Gordon
Ramsay in Hollywood.

Chapter 8
Here We Go Again. . 93

Me and Mom before
surgery for a new port.

Chapter 9
Living Now and for the Future 99

Pace Yourself. 104

Look at What's Happening Now. 105

Doing My Podcast 109

Future Plans 111

David, me, and Dad at
the pumpkin farm.

Afterword by Geri Parscale . . 113

About Getting Through the Day. 115

. . . .

Appendix A
Dr. Ginn's Notes . . . 123

. . . .

Appendix B
My Cancer Treatment Timetable. 125

Chapter 1
Some Birthday Surprise

Hi, my name is Nicholas Steven Parscale, and I'm going to tell you some of the things I wish I'd known before I got cancer. The first thing is that it's probably going to be a long road. Because cancer sucks.

When some kids get cancer, they can have an operation and just get it removed. And that's that. My cancer was inoperable, so they couldn't get the tumor out. But whether they can take it out or not, cancer can come back. That's called relapsing. And that's why my story with cancer is a little longer.

Another thing you need to know up front is that you're going to get poked and prodded a lot by people at the hospital. That's all part of it too. I've had cancer for almost five years, and I've never met one of them who wasn't really, really sorry they have to do that. In fact, they're going to bend over backwards to make you feel better. These are nice people. So, what I'm saying is that you're going to be a lot better off if you just make up your mind to be positive.

There's so much to learn during your experience. For example, I like science, and there I was surrounded by all of these doctors, nurses, and technicians. Pay attention to what they're telling you, because you can look it up later and learn for yourself what's going on. Relax and let them do what they have to do. A lot of it isn't as bad as you imagine, and so it's better to just get it done.

But I'll talk about that later. First, let me go back to June of 2016, when I was just a kid, finishing the third grade and about to turn ten years old. The picture (page 1) at the beginning of this chapter shows me at the birthday party my mom and dad set up for me and my friends. It was at this fun place in the mall called, Epic Fun—where they have arcade games, Xboxes, laser tag, pizza, and race car driving simulators. It's like a Dave & Buster's on a budget. I had absolutely no idea what was coming just a few weeks later. Getting cancer was never something I'd ever thought about. You could honestly say it was the last thing on my mind.

I was kind of a football kid back then. I mean, I was "muscley." Kind of big. I'd already played cub football for a year, and my plans were to get better at it. My favorite team has always been the Kansas City Chiefs. Which makes sense when you think about it because I've lived all my life in Kansas, first, in a little town named Troy, which is in the northeast corner of the state, and now in Lawrence, which is about an hour outside of Kansas City. I also like college basketball, especially the Jayhawks from the University of Kansas, but football is my favorite.

My family is pretty normal—there's my dad, Dave, who used to sell insurance; my mom, Geri, who used to be a principal and now works with teachers; my brother, David, who's eight years older than me; four dogs; and two cats. So, as you can tell, I'm the youngest in the family, except for the dogs and cats. Even my cousins are adults.

My family likes to take trips, so after school was out that year, we went to the beach at Panama City, Florida. Panama City is at the very top of Florida on the Gulf of Mexico, in that long, skinny part they call the Panhandle. We knew about it because my mom had been there before for her work. Going to the beach, sitting in the sun, and playing in the sand as you look out over the water are some things I really like to do.

So, I'd really been looking forward to getting there as soon as we could, but I was also not feeling so good. When I was young, I liked to sit on the floor. I don't know why, but wherever we were, I'd find a place on the floor to be comfortable. And sometimes when I'd stand up, I'd get this weird feeling I called a "brain rush," where things just didn't feel right. Not exactly dizzy, but just everything in my head was moving around. It usually would go away after a few seconds, but since before this trip, my brain rushes were lasting longer and happening every time when I'd get up from the floor or even a chair.

What I've Learned

There is a real name for what I was having—not brain rush, but *head rush*. It's the medical term for when you get up fast and your blood pressure drops really fast. It can happen when the fluid that cushions your brain gets backed up. Or when people smoke and inhale nicotine. Which tells me why I never want to smoke.

When it was almost time to come home, I got to eat my favorite food in the world, big crab legs. I mean, I don't just like crab legs—I absolutely love them. So does my dad; it's his favorite too. And on this trip, to celebrate what a great time we'd had in Panama City, we went to an all-you-can-eat buffet, and I ate a huge amount of them. As many as I'd ever eaten before. Sure, we can get crab legs in Kansas—they freeze them and fly them into the grocery—but there in Florida, the crab legs are unbelievable.

In our family, we like to leave early—going to and coming back from our trips—and so the night before leaving Florida, we were all packed up and ready to leave. That way, all we had to do the next morning was jump out of bed, get dressed, and go.

The hotel was really nice and right on the beach. Mom and Dad had the big room; my brother and I slept in the room nearby with bunk beds. In the middle of the night, I got sick and threw up all over my bunk. I went next door and tapped on Mom's shoulder as she was sleeping. She got up and cleaned up everything, including me—and we went back to sleep. We thought it was just that seafood poisoning that people can get.

Anyway, the next morning as we were rushing to get to the airport, I still felt terrible. Mostly I had this bad headache that wouldn't stop. And I kept thinking that just this once, I wish I hadn't eaten so many crab legs. Maybe I'd hit my crab-leg limit, never thought that was possible!

We'd been on the plane for a while when I knew I couldn't hold it back anymore. I grabbed one of those paper bags in the seat pocket and threw up everything. I'd never used those bags before, and they were fun to use—but without feeling that bad. Mom helped me again, and the flight attendant was right there giving us some wet towels. But I kept throwing up, even though everything *had* to be out by then. Worst of all, the headache wouldn't go away. It wasn't a normal headache but like a knife stabbing me over and over behind my eye.

When the plane landed, I was still sick. Throwing up anything they tried to give me, even water. The pain in my head kept getting worse and worse.

Mom said we all probably just needed a vacation from a vacation. That sort of made sense. Anyway, I slept all the first day we got back home. The following day, it wasn't any worse, but it also wasn't any better—just the same. So, Mom took me to see our family doctor.

Dr. Johanning thought that I had migraines—which I've since learned is a type of severe headache that can also cause you to get sick to your stomach and dizzy. I felt all those things, so it made sense. My mom was surprised because of my age, but he said kids can get them too. They gave me two shots, one in each arm, right inside my elbow—and then he said, "If this doesn't work, come back tomorrow."

Here's a surprise—those shots didn't do a thing. The next day, I felt as bad as ever, so we went back to his office. And the doctor there sent us right to the emergency room at Lawrence Memorial Hospital, where those doctors ran a CT scan.

A CT scan is where you lie flat on this little table that slides into a tunnel-like machine, that sort of looks like a thick, white doughnut when you look straight at it. The CT scan is similar to a camera, and it takes pictures of whatever is the problem inside your body. It didn't hurt and wasn't even scary at all. At this point, I was up for anything that would just make me feel better.

Later, the doctor told Mom something like, "Don't freak out. Nicholas has fluid on his brain. We're not sure why. It could be a lot of different things, but we want you to take him to Children's Mercy Hospital in Kansas City, where they can figure out what's causing this."

Up until then, my mom had been pretty much her normal self, but I could tell something was different. Right away she called my dad to tell him where we were going.

This was my first time in an ambulance, but early on, they gave me something to sleep and so I don't remember the trip. Mom said they didn't even run the siren or the red lights, so I didn't miss anything. When we got there, I woke up for a little bit and saw that my dad and my brother had showed up too.

At Children's Mercy, a place I would come to know very well over the next four years, some of the nurses helped me change my clothes into a hospital gown, and I had the first of many MRIs. An MRI is a lot like the CT scan, only bigger. You're still lying down on the table, and you still slide into the machine, which is like a big white tube. The people there are called technicians, and they said it would give us even better pictures.

What I've Learned

It turns out that the MRI is the updated version of the CT scan. The CT scan uses the old-style X-ray to show your insides; an MRI uses a magnetic field and radio waves. The pictures are in color and look like pizza slices. I'm guessing they use the CT scan first to screen out the stuff that can be fixed right away.

I've gotten used to them, but I must admit to you that I didn't like the first MRI. First, they take a lot longer—you have to hold very still in one position so the images won't be blurred. Sometimes they will give you medicine to make you calm or sleepy, and sometimes they will give you headphones to listen to calming music. There are lights inside, but you have to keep reminding yourself that you can't just get up and out. After a while, you do get used to it.

It took us all day, but they finally gave me a room in a section called 2 Henson at Children's Mercy Pediatric Intensive Care Unit—they call it the PICU, which I think is a funny name. Get it? Pick You?

It had been over twelve hours since waking up that morning in Lawrence. I was exhausted, and all I wanted to do was get to sleep. Then a surgeon came into the room and asked my parents to go talk with him somewhere else. I knew he was a surgeon because one of my favorite shows is *Grey's Anatomy,* and he had on one of those surgical scrub outfits they wear. I figured they were talking about me, but I was so tired, I went to sleep anyway.

The Monster Shows Up

Later, my mom told me that he had shown them the MRI images of my brain and he'd told them that I had a blockage in the system of fluid that surrounds the brain and spinal cord. I had never thought of this before, but I've since learned that your brain kind of "floats" in a fluid that feeds it, removes all the toxins and waste materials, and then as an extra bonus, cushions it from being bumped around when you move or get hit in the head. Like me playing football. That's what the fluid is supposed to do anyway.

Well, my tumor was right where this fluid drains into the spine. I think of it like a bean caught in a soda straw, clogging up the whole system, causing the fluid to back up, and causing my brain to swell inside my skull. Which certainly explained the horrible headaches.

Long story short, this whole blockage was right in the middle of my head—near my pineal gland. And it was cancer. That's why they call my particular cancer a *pineoblastoma*. At first, they called it *glioblastoma*. You're going to hear a lot of big words you've never heard before, but don't worry. There are people who talk like that at hospitals. Glioblastoma is the big category, like the NFL, and pineoblastoma is a specific team, like the Chiefs.

What I've Learned

Everybody has a pineal gland. They're still not sure about all that it does, but my doctor told me they think it helps you go to sleep.

Early the next morning, they moved me to another floor, which turned out to be the oncology floor where kids with cancer stay. That's so they have the right medicines, hospital staff, and equipment they need for cancer all in one place. Mom and Dad came into my room to tell me that I was going to have the surgery.

I remember Mom said, "Bubby (that's her nickname for me), they're going to make you feel better."

And I was so ready for that!

I said, "Good. Let's do it then! Let's get this tumor out!"

Then the nurses came in and prepared me for surgery. They were very nice, and they shaved most of the hair on the top of my head (which was weird) and gave me some medicine to help me relax. It makes you feel pretty groggy.

When you get in the operating room, the lights are bright and there are people you've never seen before—but there's no reason for you to be scared. These people are the operating nurses, the surgeons, and the anesthesiologists, and they all know what they're doing. The surgeon does the actual cutting and opening you up—in my case, it was my skull. The *anesthesiologist* is the doctor who keeps you totally asleep so you can't feel anything. So, don't worry, if you think somebody opening up your skull and getting into your brain hurts, because you don't feel a thing. In fact, my cousin, Garrett, told me later your brain can't even feel pain anyway. That kind of scientific thing I think is very interesting.

At the start of the surgery, they drilled two holes in my head—one in the front, just above my forehead a little off to the right side, and another one farther back. That let them stick things in, like this little light, and move in and over and down to look at everything in there.

First, I have to tell you a bit about your brain, which is very complicated. The doctors use the images they get from the MRI scan to tell them how to move around once they're inside and what to do. Turns out your brain is soft and kind of squishy. I've seen people on TV making pastry, and it's like if your brain was folded in on itself over and over, so it's got all these layers and sections that do special things. Anyway, like I said, the pineal gland is in the very center and right where the fluids go down into your spine.

What I've Learned

Your brain is made up of two halves called *hemispheres*, and each of those halves has five sections called *lobes*. Each lobe does its own special job. One moves your body, and another one controls how your personality is, what you remember, and so on. Like I said, it is complicated.

The good news is that when they got in there, they were able to make another drain hole to bypass the tumor blockage and allow all the fluid to flow like it's supposed to. That relieved the pressure inside my head. I guess it also let them see things better.

When the drainage problem was solved, they took out a little bit of the tumor and sent it to the lab to be tested. This procedure is called a *biopsy*. Then they closed up everything and mostly put my skull back together. I was still asleep through all of that, and when I woke up, I was back in my hospital room.

The next day and for a little while after the surgery, there was this 8–10-inch tube coming out of the second hole on the top of my head. After they took the tube out, for a couple of weeks later, as the wound started to heal over, there was this growth that would come out of the hole just like the end of a hot dog. It would start off small, and then it would get bigger and bigger—like an inch or two. You could touch it a little, and it would go right back in. Real quick. Sounds wild, but it didn't hurt. My dad and I joked that it was the alien trying to get out, like in that movie where the alien comes out of that guy's chest. We watch movies a lot together, and I thought that was pretty funny.

What I've Learned

When you have surgery, they can't always just sew things back up. It depends on how deep they go and if they take things out or put things in. Usually, they want to leave it open a little so it can heal from the inside out. They put in tubes so the surgery site or wound drains, and they can keep it clean. That doesn't last too long.

Later, I met Dr. Ginn, a really great doctor who is my *oncologist*. He wasn't the surgeon; that was a different person. The oncologist is the doctor in charge of your cancer treatments and making sure that everybody does the best they can for you. Dr. Ginn came into my room and sat on the edge of my bed. He started off by asking me if I knew what was wrong.

Then he told me that I was sick and that I had cancer. He told me about how the surgery went and why they couldn't remove the tumor in my brain. They already knew that it had started to grow and where it had spread out to, but with the little sample from the biopsy, they learned more about what kind of tumor it was—rare— and a grade four out of four. They found it, and that was the best part. But the bottom line was, even trying to remove it like it was could make it worse. That meant they needed to try some other procedures instead.

He said, "We're gonna treat it. And we're gonna make it better. Everybody's gonna help you."

But what I remember most was what he told me next. Something very important and something I've thought about since.

"Sometimes," he said, "You're gonna cry, and you're gonna be sad. Sometimes Mom's gonna cry. Dad's gonna cry. Brother's gonna cry. And I'm gonna cry too. But we're all going to do the best we can."

And he was right. Still, you also get to celebrate when there's good news. Not "party, party, whoop, whoop" or anything, but the good news *really does* feel good.

I looked at Mom and Dad. They were smiling and giving me the thumbs-up, but I could tell they'd been crying already. And I thought, "Well, I'm glad Dr. Ginn gave it to me straight." He didn't treat me like I was too young to be told the truth. I liked that. I thought, "We'll just have to deal with it then." One more hurdle to jump over. At least my headache was gone for now.

Over the next few days, lots of other people from my family showed up to visit and bring me balloons, toys, and things. Even our priest, Father Mick, came to talk to me, my parents, and my brother. He's a great guy too, and I'll tell you more about him later. Actually, I've said that a lot because there's a lot more of my story to tell.

They had to let my surgery heal, and that took a while. I was in Children's Mercy for about forty-five days. Then one of the other procedures Dr. Ginn mentioned meant chemotherapy—*chemo* for short. I got an implant in my chest, which has this plastic thing called a *port* where they can stick in a needle to take out blood and stuff, but mainly it's where they put the chemo in. My hair fell out. I got pretty skinny. And it makes me itchy. I'll tell you all about that in chapter 4 (page 31).

I had radiation too, at the same time. During that procedure, I got to wear this cool plastic mesh helmet, which I still have. Then I got better! Then I had a relapse.

All the while, I've been keeping up with my friends, playing video games like Minecraft, painting—I love to paint—seeing my cousins, going fishing, and sometimes traveling to fun places to meet really interesting people—including Gordon Ramsay, the famous chef on TV! He's really nice in person, not prickly like he sometimes seems on TV.

I've had at least a dozen more MRIs. Only now, I get to pick a movie to watch, and that really helps with being bored or wanting to move around. My dad always jokes before I go to one of the MRIs, "Did you study hard for the test?" And when I'm finished, he'll say, "You did good on that test!"

And I want to start a foundation called Chemo, Kitties, and Canines. I thought of that name by myself, so I can get it trade-marked. I told you we have four dogs—Briar, Jingle, Loki, and Rosy—and two cats—Sweet'ems and Mr. Fox. I got Rosy (she's a blonde Labrador) the second Christmas I had cancer. She knows I'm sick, and she helps me up the stairs if I need it. Kids with cancer get a lot of stuffed animals, and those are nice, but I think having the real thing—a real dog or a real cat—is the best. And these should be rescue animals. More about this idea in chapter 9.

Because of Mark Evans DM, or *The Deal-Maker*, a great man I met through a friend, I get to make a podcast, where I interview lots of interesting people about their lives and how they help others stay positive. If you want to check out my podcast, *Nick the Brave: Chemo, Kitties, and Canines*, you can listen to it wherever podcasts are available: Apple Podcasts, Audible, Spotify, the Podcast Factory, and more.

I've had another relapse, more rounds of chemo, and I've missed out on a couple of experimental trials. Moving forward. But it still sucks.

I'll let you in on all the details later, but for now, it's enough to know that at this point in my story—when I first got diagnosed—everyone in my family was pretty freaked out. That's something else important you'll need to learn how to deal with, but again, that'll be in another chapter.

My doctor and the people at Children's Mercy used to call me Nick the Brave. I never thought that I was particularly really brave.

Certainly not braver than anybody I'd ever heard of. I knew from the very beginning that God gave me cancer so that other younger kids wouldn't have to get it—maybe that was because they couldn't take it.

Now, after all my experiences with cancer, I want to write a book that will be a guide for other kids like me. You're reading this and finding yourself in the same situation. Your cancer isn't going to be exactly like mine, and your experiences are going to be unique to you. But I still really hope there are some things in here that you can use along the way to always stay positive.

So, let's get started.

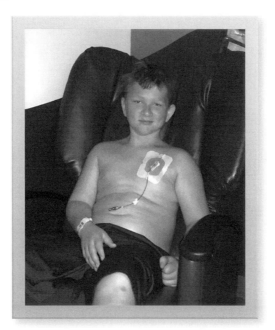

This is me getting some chemo. The port is implanted in my chest. One end of the tube goes through the port and deep inside a vein. They put the chemicals in through the other end.

Chapter 2
The Best Medicine of All

Since I'm writing this book to let you know what I wish I knew before I got cancer, it only seems fair to give you some of the most important things right off the bat.

So here they are:

- First thing. Keep a positive attitude! My parents say—and they're right—it is the best medicine of all. Plus, no bad side effects either.

- Surround yourself with positive people and positive energy; I don't care about negativity of any kind. In fact, when I'm around negative people, I just leave. I don't put up with negativity.

- You will have many opportunities to make new friends and go to new places. Enjoy everything that you can.

- Pay attention to everything all around as you go through it. First, it's your life; you should be interested. And second, there is a lot of new stuff you can learn through science. (That last one is up to you, of course.)

- Pay attention to what the doctors and nurses are saying. They are only trying to do everything they can to help you.

- ○ Trust yourself. Listen to yourself too.
- ○ Tell someone when you need to. Tell the doctors, tell your parents, tell anybody if something is wrong or bothering you. Tell them if it hurts too much. Nobody knows what you're feeling better than you do.
- ○ You will see kids and adults around you being afraid, but don't be scared yourself. And when you can, try making them feel okay. It might even make you feel better too.

And to everybody else, I would say: just treat us like you would any regular kid. We're still here. Be honest if things are bad or something is going to hurt. That's something you can get ready for! Plus, kids are tougher than most adults think. One time when I was really little, my dad wouldn't let me watch a scary monster movie that he had rented. So, I had to stay in the other room hearing the screams, explosions, and gasps coming from the TV and him—which was way worse than bloody scenes or anything else in the movie. When you're honest about the cancer from the start, it will be easier to trust each other in the tough times ahead. And that can be important because sometimes kids feel like they're to blame for something they didn't really have anything to do with.

Oh, and if you're seeing a kid with cancer for the first time, try not to stare. Nobody likes to be stared at after all.

Let Me Rewind a Little

Just before I was born, Mom had a hard time; so, she had to have surgery to deliver me earlier than they thought. They call that a *cae-sarean section*. I wasn't able to breathe by myself, so they put me in intensive care for three days. Those three days must have been hard on everybody. On the actual night they all started planning how to transport me from the local hospital in Atchison, Kansas, straight to Children's Mercy in Kansas City—that very night—I decided to breathe on my own. That's when my parents started calling me a miracle child. One of my dad's friends even called me Lucky, and he still does. Mom said that I must have heard the doctors and nurses talking about it and so I decided, "Okay, now it's time for me to breathe on my own." Maybe. Who knows? I've always kind of been like that. Just tell me the next thing that has to be done, and I get started.

How to Stay Positive

I decided to make a list of things I've learned about how anyone can practice being positive.

Be on the lookout for something you can do for somebody else.

For example, not too long ago, I gave my friend a rose. She was very sad about her aunt who was sick. I've given flowers to multiple people, and they all really seem to like them, no matter what the reason.

My dad taught me that on the last day of my first round of radiation. On the way to the clinic, we went to a funeral home flower shop. By that I mean, they sold those big wreaths people send to funeral homes. I know that because they had big bunches of flowers all over the place to show how nice they could put things together. So, I asked them, "What are these big ones for?" That's when I learned that there are all kinds of special flowers you give for every kind of occasion. Birthdays, funerals, leaving your job parties, really flowers for anything you can think of, but mostly this place was good at flowers for funerals. Anyway, we got a whole bunch of yellow roses to take to the nurses and technicians at the clinic—and for the receptionist, who was always especially happy to see me. That's when I learned that everybody likes to get flowers. Boy, girl, man, woman, everybody. It doesn't matter. Even if you think they would never even look at a flower. People do like them.

Focus on how other people feel when they are trying to help out.

Remember that most people, family, friends, and even total strangers don't always know the right thing to say even when they want to. They all feel really bad that you have cancer. In some ways, that's because, like I said before, it sucks, and they can see that. And also, because cancer scares them too—which I totally get.

Most of the time when they first meet you, people don't really know how to ask you about it—the cancer, I mean. Especially, if they've never had cancer or had one of their kids have it. Most of the time, this comes out in what I call "babying." They don't mean anything bad by it, but they can talk to you just like you're a little baby sometimes.

Don't get me wrong. Sometimes you like to be babied, I mean like when you've really been sick or throwing up and stuff. But sometimes that gets annoying. From the second I got sick, I was babied by *some* people until I got a little better, and then I could speak for myself more. I'm not saying I shouldn't have been babied when I was really a baby, but I'm fourteen years old now!

Times like that can be weird, but I think you should try to get over it. That's just my opinion; it's totally up to you. But usually when people do things like that, it's because they just feel bad for you, they want to help, and they don't know what to say—that's all.

Here's what I do when it happens—just smile and listen. Sometimes, only if I feel like it, I'll make a joke or talk about other fun things so they can relax. In the end, it makes me feel good inside that they were trying to show me that they cared about what I was going through.

Mainly, you want to see when people are trying.

It's like when I first played football. I was a lineman, and after just watching a play, I still didn't know what to do. All the coaches said at first was to stop the guy in front of you—put your forefingers out straight, and then put them in the other guy's armpits to stop him. So, I did. But after that, I didn't know what else to do. I mean, now what? The coaches had to *see* how I stopped the guy in front of me and then tell me what to do next. Things take real-life practice to learn.

You'll see the same thing when you're in the hospital and all the student nurses and student technicians come into your room. They were told what to do in school. They probably even watched videos about taking blood and sticking tubes into people, but they still hadn't tried it on a real patient. And if they don't practice, they'll never get it right. So, you have to be patient and understand that they're trying the best they can.

Once when I told this lady I played guard on our football team, she said that was too bad because they never can score.

"Well, sure we can," I said. "If I'm there when the ball comes!"

The ball can come to you at any time, and you have to try to be ready.

It doesn't help anything to be negative when the ball does come to you.

Being positive just feels better than being negative.

I like having fun and being around people. Lots of times, it's my friends and the new people I meet who keep me going. I like being friends with almost all of the new people I meet. I like talking to anybody and learning about them. It makes me feel good. And when I'm feeling good, people say I can really work the crowd. But that's not my goal; I just like it.

One group of people I met at the Kansas City Renaissance Festival is called the Widow's Brethren in the West. I think that's a funny

name. This is a club of people who like dressing up in medieval cos-
tumes and like mythical characters. At the festival, I wore a pirate
costume, and my name was Shark Tooth. My costume included a
wooden knife with a real shark's tooth on it and a walking stick with
a dragon's head at the top. Then a few months later, they all dressed
like pirates and marched down the street in my neighborhood to
present me with a parchment scroll granting me a commission in
their crew as Captain Shark Tooth. They also gave me this great hat
with feathers and a real periscope! That was a lot of fun. The next
festival will be Labor Day of 2021 in Bonner Springs, Kansas. I sure
would love to go back and visit then.

Me and a crew of pirates I ran into.

Look for things that give you a sense of success.

Turns out I really like diamond painting. It's like putting together
a mosaic with little pieces of plastic and glue. Sort of like a paint by
number, but a lot harder. I like it because it takes lots of concentration

and, at the end, you can look at it and be proud and say to yourself, "I did this!"

Keep track of who you really are.

Being confident in myself is something that comes easy to me now, but I have had to work at it during the last four years. It wasn't always easy, but I just keep looking ahead. I always say that in the long run, everything will be fine. If I get hurt, everything will be fine. If I get sicker, everything will still be fine in the end.

Have I changed over the last four years? Of course, I'm four years older, and I'm twice as big, not a little kid anymore. But I've changed inside too. Four years ago, people used to think that I was a tough guy, maybe even a little mean or rude sometimes. Never to little kids, but if some guy would come up to me and be mean or try to push me around, I could take care of myself. That was part of who I was. But that's definitely not my personality anymore!

When the cancer came and I realized how tough it was going to be to fight, I knew that one of the first things I was going to have to do was change my own attitude. I needed every bit of my energy to go against the cancer, not other people. It just wasn't worth it to fight or argue or even be mad at people—usually for things they can't change anyway.

And so that's how I decided to always be a good person, like at clinic and stuff. Because if you fuss and cuss and roll about, it's not gonna get done. It's only gonna take longer, then get you and everybody else upset, and probably hurt even more. You've got to realize that out of all the tough steps you have to go through, if it's lying there without moving during the radiation, or trying not to be scared when you're in the MRI machine, or taking all the needles— and believe me, I hate needles as much as anyone—still, 95 percent of these things are going to help you in the long run.

Having cancer makes you see what's really important and what isn't. Other things aren't quite so awful after all. For example, my dad has this thing where his eyelids droop; it's just a thing he inherited. He drove me to the clinic for my treatments on days when Mom had to travel for her job, but his eyelid thing started to affect his sight. So, one time when Mom was back, he went to get his eye surgery to pull the droopy lids up. He walked into the doctor's office, ready to get surgery on his eyelids, and he heard this adult woman screaming her head off because they were going to stick a needle in her eye. I mean, isn't that what you would expect if you're at the eye surgeon getting your eyes operated on? What do you think they do in there anyway?

And my dad told the nurse, "I go to the clinic with my son for his cancer treatments, and I hear little four-year-olds who don't scream that loud."

Stuff like that puts things in perspective.

I still slip up sometimes, but now when I see somebody acting up or being mean, I'm more likely to get where that's coming from. When I see somebody acting up like that, I feel bad for them, especially the little kids. But whoever it is, I try to remember that maybe he or she had a bad day, or maybe he or she was even in pain or hurting somehow. You don't know what other people are dealing with. Mostly people are just scared that they don't know what is coming. So, in that way, I would say that learning how to be positive while fighting cancer has made me a better person. Definitely better able to deal with stuff.

And to me, the most important part of learning that lesson is to only surround myself with positive people and positive thoughts.

They Say I'm an Old Soul

People in my family say that I'm an old soul because I like talking to old people. Really, I just think they're interesting. When I was born, my parents and older brother and all my cousins were a lot older than me, because I was kind of a surprise baby. I've always been around older people, and I like them. I think they're nice and they know a lot of interesting things to talk about. They've seen things that aren't around anymore.

For a long time, my mom's mom, Grandma Lillian, used to take care of me after school. Then my dad's mom died of cancer when she was old. Just a few months later, Grandma Lillian went too. I never knew my grandfathers because they had both died before I was born.

When I was a little kid, we had a next-door neighbor named Mrs. Smith. She was like a grandmother age, and I loved going over to her house to talk to her. We lived on the same road that my mom grew up on, and her mom, Grandma Lillian, used to live on her farm just up the road from Mrs. Arlene Smith. Mrs. Smith had cows and a huge garden that I loved playing in. As long as I told my mom where I was going, I could go over there anytime I wanted and sit on the porch and talk to her. She lived to be ninety-seven, which is pretty old. She talked to me and listened when I talked. She was always giving me orange slices and other stuff to eat.

Another thing I know about myself is that I have what's called Catholic guilt. Once, Mrs. Smith's nephew, Greg, took me fishing, and by total crazy accident, I got a fishhook stuck in his eyebrow! God was looking out for us that day because I didn't hook his eyeball. That would have been terrible. I would have felt very, very guilty and upset because as I said, I have Catholic guilt.

When you're raised Catholic you pay attention to how you look at things and go about life. It's how you're raised. My favorite priest is Father Mick Mulvany. I told you in the last chapter how he was there for all of us when I first got sick.

Me and Father Mick. He's a very positive person.

My family has a strong faith in God also. I feel it in my heart even though there are some things I believe in and some things I don't. Mainly, I'm a science guy. Still, I definitely believe there is a God even though I don't really pray much. Grandma Lillian and Mom always prayed a lot.

Grandma Lillian was a great lady. I remember she couldn't see anybody without her makeup and her lipstick on—nobody! Didn't matter who. If they just showed up and she wasn't ready, they'd have to wait outside. And when we'd all go to church together, it was fun to mess around a little bit just to make her ticked off, like how me and my brother would pretend to hit each other. But I knew when to stop it and straighten up. She wasn't alive when I first got cancer, and I think that's a good thing because it would have hurt her very much. She once had breast cancer, so while she would have understood, she also would have been really sad.

Now, only if you want to—make a list of the things that really describe you. Get rid of the negative parts, and spend your time with the positives. That way you can let yourself be happy with who that person is.

Chapter 3
What Is Cancer, Anyway?

My dad says a real man never punches a woman. That's just not done, no matter what. That makes sense to me because, generally, men are bigger and stronger than most women. Not always, but usually you can hurt them more than they can hurt you back. I have seen some mixed gender martial arts or self-defense shows on TV—and they don't count because the women signed up for it. But once we were watching a TV show set in a hospital, and one of the characters was a woman who was *just pretending* to have cancer! Faking it just because she wanted the attention. Now to me, that's a punchable offense. To me, the one thing you don't ever fake is cancer. When I think about it, I don't think that's something a kid would ever really do. I think kids are more honest.

Me, 2016, just getting started.

I can't tell you scientifically what cancer is, which makes total sense, because I'm not a doctor yet! And besides, you should only listen to what your oncologist says about it anyway. I mean, I get other regular people telling me all the time what they think it is. And they don't really know. You just have to take that stuff and forget it.

Doctor Ginn told me you can get cancer all over your body— except the three main places you can't get it, or it's probably not going to be there, are in your hair, your fingernails, and your heart. Just one of those weird facts I really like. Like how hot water freezes faster than lukewarm water—scientists think they might sort of know why, but they aren't totally sure. Guess my point is there's still a lot to learn.

Me and my cancer dream team. Dr. Ginn, my oncologist, and Diana Healy, my nurse practitioner.

What I've Learned

People at the hospital said that cells are, like, microscopic building blocks that make up everything in your body. I thought of LEGO®. And while they do different things for different parts of your body, like your hair, stomach, eyes, brain, everything—each one carries little bits of information that make you who you are.

They come in different shapes from little doughnut O's, like blood cells, to ones like nerve cells with long, skinny tails and things that look like arms. Cells in fat and muscle can shrink or get bigger, and you can see that for yourself on somebody, even without a microscope. Lots of cells multiply—and that's how you grow up and turn into an adult.

Cancer cells also grow, but just way too fast, because they overtake everything else you need. They're like weeds in the garden. Or cockroaches. Or little monsters. That might be okay if they did something good, but they don't because they're just bad. They destroy good things in their path. Like a selfish monster, that cares only about itself.

A *tumor* is a big group of cells getting together, and doctors sometimes call it a *mass*. Not all tumors are cancerous; they can just be masses of cells, and doctor's call those *benign* (which is a fancy word for harmless). Benign tumors usually don't hurt anything; the doctors just watch them to be sure.

There are over a hundred different kinds of cancers, and everybody has a few cancer cells popping up all the time that don't end up hurting you. There are lots of reasons for that. Some of the reasons doctors know, some they don't.

Most of the time, your body kills cancer cells with a weapons system called your *immune system*. It's made up of special cells, a few organs (like your tonsils), and other special organs called glands. All of these are like your personal warriors. But sometimes one tiny little cancer cell can get through—that usually happens in old people, maybe because their weapons are old and they kind of wear out. That would make sense. But it can also happen for little kids. As we know.

It sounds pretty random to me. Kind of like when you draw a bad hand of cards in a poker game.

Dr. Ginn has added his notes at the end of my book (page 123) that tells you some of the details about the kind of cancer and treatments I've had.

I know this may seem too short for a real chapter, but like Forrest Gump says, "That's all I have to say about that."

Chapter 4
Going Into Whatever's Up Next

I've been in the hospital a lot these past four years. Once it was for over forty-five days straight, but usually I'd be in the hospital for a week, then out for a while, then back in again. Father Mick says that everybody has a different journey, so everybody's treatment is different. That makes sense, but I think there are some things that happen to almost all of us. So, I've put together a few main tips that I wish somebody had told me when this all started.

Trusting Your Team Helps a Lot

When you first go into the hospital, you may not know how long you're going to be there, and no, it's not going to be anything like being at home. Don't let that bother you. As soon as you're admitted into the hospital, you'll be assigned to a team that will care for you. My team always had three main people who were in charge: an oncologist, a nurse practitioner, and a social worker. I already told you that my oncologist is Dr. Ginn, and he is the main guy in charge of my cancer treatment overall. He is amazing. He's usually dressed up with a bow tie on, and he always makes me laugh every time, no matter what. He even knows some of my dad's friends.

He's not going to be my lifelong doctor though because once I turn twenty-one, I can't go to Children's Mercy anymore, which will be kind of sad. But he said we can always be friends even when I have a new team. Remember when I told you how he said, "Mom will cry, Dad will cry, your brother will cry, and I will cry"? Well, he did a little once.

Sometime during the second year I had cancer—I can't remember exactly when—my family and I were at an art fair in Kansas City when we saw an artist who had done a drawing of a Converse sneaker with an iguana lizard crawling up over the side. Now, I personally *love* Converse. I wear them all of the time; they are definitely my favorite and most comfortable shoe. And Dr. Ginn had told me that he likes them too. Somehow, we also found out that we both liked iguanas. Well, Mom bought that drawing, and we gave it to him. When he got it, he teared up, just a little, because he really loved it. He thanked me a lot, and he still has it on his office wall.

My nurse practitioner is Diana Healy, and her job is to help Dr. Ginn, make treatment plans, and coordinate all the other people on the team. You saw a picture of them both (page 28) in the last chapter.

My social worker is Caroline Gill. The social worker's job is to help you and your family with non-medical things they might need, like finding a place to stay if you're from out of town. They can connect you to groups and foundations that are looking to help out kids with cancer. One time a group helped us get more feeding tubes when we couldn't find the right ones. Hallmark, the greeting card company, is based in Kansas City, Missouri, and they donate a lot of toys and stuffed animals, also games and fun things, to the hospital. Companies everywhere do that. And so do the Marines with Toys for Tots. The social worker can pull those things together—so the right family gets the right help.

It's up to you, but I made friends with as many of the team members as possible because they're only there to help you and your family; that's really all they want to do.

One big bonus I had was when my cousin Garrett got to be one of the people helping me in the hospital. He's a respiratory therapist.

What I've Learned

A *respiratory therapist* is someone who helps people who have trouble breathing. This turns out to be even more important during the COVID-19 pandemic because people with COVID-19 can't always catch their breath by themselves.

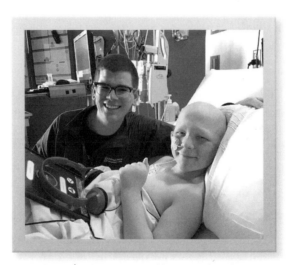

Me and my cousin Garrett, who's a traveling respiratory therapist. That means he goes to lots of different hospitals, helping people who need him.

These relationships are all important, and you want to speak up to your parents or guardians when you really, really like someone on your hospital team. And even if you ever run into a doctor you don't like, you should say so. That matters too. Even if everybody else is telling you this is a really great doctor, trust your instincts. You have a right to your opinion. And I think your family and the others on the hospital team should listen to you like mine do.

One time when I was in the hospital, I came in contact with a pharmacist's assistant who seemed to want to baby me. She would come into my room every once in a while, giving out the medicine—meds we call it. And this one time, she was bound and determined that I was to be taking this certain kind. But Dr. Ginn had just told me he was going to stop that medication. I always try to remember their names, so I knew. And no matter how nicely or many times I told her, she wouldn't believe me. I kept saying, "No, that was wrong." And she still wouldn't believe me. Finally, Mom had to step in and tell her very strongly that I wasn't taking it until the pharmacist checked again with the doctor. So, while as a general rule you should be patient and not annoyed when the hospital people say to do something, there can be times when you have to stand up for yourself. When you know, or you really feel like something's not right, the people working with you will double-check it, just to be sure. After all, they don't want to get things wrong either.

The Monkey in My Chair Program

At Children's Mercy Hospital, they have a special program that was started by some parents for their daughter, Chloe. They were from Kansas too, but it's not just here. They have it all over the country, so you might want to ask if your hospital has something like it. They give you a special stuffed monkey to take with you everywhere you go. Then they have a bigger stuffed monkey with his own backpack that they send to your school. He sits there in your chair at your desk, and the teacher can explain to the other kids that you're just gone for a little bit and that you'll be back. They call it the Monkey in My Chair. I named my monkey Theo. There's also a book so your teacher can explain to your friends what's going on. That way they don't worry too much about you. My mom used to be a teacher, so she looked it over and said it was really a great idea.

Me and Theo. Going into whatever's up next.

You're Going to Get Poked and Prodded

Poked and prodded is what old people call it when somebody—even somebody you don't know very well—just fusses over you, checking this and that. Giving you shots, telling you to drink something, and not always telling you what or why. It was something that I really didn't like when I first got cancer. I didn't like being touched so much. And I didn't always want to sit still for long times either. But I had to get used to it because you get so much of that in the hospital. It would be great if there were another way, but there isn't yet.

And don't be surprised at how *many different* people come in and out of your room. For me, it was about thirty—not all at once, but throughout the time I was there. Doctors, nurses, respiratory therapists, people bringing food, and sometimes just other people checking in to see how things are going. Sometimes people will come with carts filled with toys, card games, and books, and you get to pick a surprise or something. They also have lots of crafts, painting supplies, and things so you have something to do when you're bored.

There will be a TV, and, in my case, we even had a PlayStation to use. Everybody at the hospital is very nice—they all try to make you feel better—but I didn't always know what they were there for. I think they should always tell you.

I remember one of the nurses who called me her boyfriend. She was kidding with me, but every time she would come into my room, she would say, "Hi, Boyfriend, how are you today?" Then she would check my temperature, pulse rate, blood pressure, how fast I was breathing, and a couple of other things. They call those measurements your *vitals*—meaning you have to have them to be alive, I guess. She was fun, and I always liked it when she came in. And she always explained everything to me. I think it's better to know—but you might be different, and that's ok.

There will be some times when you will be dealing with students who are just learning their jobs at the hospital. So, you may have a nurse bring in a student nurse to learn how to take a blood sample from you. And the students may really be bad at doing a certain thing, like they can't get the needle to go directly into your vein. They miss it, maybe even a couple of times. It's hard not to squirm or be annoyed, especially when they're not very good at it. But you can't complain or yell at them because everybody has to learn sometime. Remember, the more experienced graduate nurse will be right there watching and making sure nothing really bad will happen.

Of course, things have changed a lot with COVID-19. Outside the hospital, I have to be careful not to let people touch me at all or get too close, but most don't try anymore. And that's understandable. I've never been a *germaphobe* (that's somebody who is afraid of germs), but you've got to be super careful when you have cancer because you're in the high-risk group. At least you don't have to worry about that in the hospital or clinic because the people there are pros, and they know all the right ways to protect everybody there.

They Like It When You Eat

When you're in the hospital, they are always trying to get you to eat something, and they offer all kinds of treats and things—the menu is endless. Almost anything you want, they'll bring it to you like Sprite. No candy because they don't have it. They have fruit snacks, granola bars, apple juice, cranberry juice, any kind of juice you want, though not strawberry juice and mango juice but you know, normal kinds of juice. And if you can wait a little for it, there's a cafeteria with something like room service in a hotel. It's good food.

One of my favorites used to be SpaghettiOs. That was then. Now, they've kind of been ruined for me because they remind me of being in the hospital and feeling bad. Don't get me wrong, I could eat it if my life depended on it. But now, you'll never hear me say, "I want SpaghettiOs!" That is definitely not what comes to mind.

They kept all of the snacks in a closet at the nurses' station, and one night one of the other guys on my floor figured out how to get into it. We never told anybody, and after he left, I didn't go in there without one of the nurses. It was really their room.

My room had a TV, a bathroom, some chairs, and a little bed where my parents could sit with me or one of them could even spend the night.

Chemotherapy

I first had surgery for my cancer on July 10, 2016, the day after we found out about it. Then I went home to recover, and early that August, we started the treatments. The first step was another surgery to put the port in my chest so they could easily inject the chemicals. When you have cancer, the main reason you go back to the hospital is to get treatments to catch and kill the cancer cells before they can grow and take over. For me, that usually happened in one of the hospital clinics. The clinic can be in a special part of the hospital, or it can be in its own building in another part of town.

Every day, Monday through Friday, we would leave early in the morning and drive an hour to the Children's Mercy Hospital to have chemotherapy. We'd go to one side of the *hematology* floor that has a waiting room and another room where they take a sample of your blood to check on how things are coming along.

Over the weeks or months that you will be getting the chemo (and you'll have your own special schedule), you'll have to check back with the doctor or the hospital many times to have your blood taken. You'll probably be sitting in a chair with an armrest that pulls up from the side so you can stretch out your arm to give them a clear shot at the vein on the inside of your elbow.

What I've Learned

The person who takes your blood sample (they call it *blood work* or *drawing blood*) is a phlebotomist. This can be a nurse or a special technician. It's an old word from Greece, and back then they'd take out your blood with bloodsucking worms called leeches. Cool.

So, when it's time to take some of your blood, the phlebotomist will have this little kit with sterile gloves that comes in a package. They clean your arm with alcohol and then stick the needle in. If you're afraid of the needle, ask them to show it to you first. That can let you get used to it. Or maybe you're someone who doesn't want to see, whatever works for you. When they're done, they put a dressing over it and some tape. It gets to be pretty normal and doesn't hurt as much after a while.

If all you're getting is blood work, you might get to go home then. But when I'd be at the hospital for chemo, after they took my blood, we'd meet with the doctor to answer any questions before moving to the second side of the hospital floor where they *access the port*, which means to put in the chemicals.

In chapter 1, there's a picture of me sitting in a big, black stuffed chair about to get the chemo (page 13). They have these big stuffed chairs because you do have to sit there for a while. You can see on my chest what looks like a clear press-and-seal plastic bandage holding the port in place. The port is the solid white plastic bit in the middle, and it's attached to a thin tube that goes into a big vein over your heart. The ports can be in different shapes; my first ones were circle shaped, and then later they went to one that was diamond shaped.

What I've Learned

When chemicals or even water are put in your veins, it's mostly in your arms, but I've seen them put it in a guy's neck. Because you have chemo so often, the veins in your arm would get messed up, so that's why they use a port. It's called *intravenous* or *IV* for short. It's Latin (an old language from Italy and the church); the first part says *into* and the second says *vein* in English. I think you can pretty much see that.

The first thing they have to do is clean out the port. And that's where the big needles come in. I sure don't like needles, but it's the only way they can get you the chemo. Those needles are a lot longer than the ones they use for the blood tests. Sometimes 10 inches, and I often get a 12-inch needle. The first one uses a pullback system called a syringe. That gets any gunk out of the port so it's all clean. The nurse uses a cold spray to numb my chest. That helps, because this isn't a fun part. Sometimes they had a diamond shaped needle that they would have to put in at an angle. If you want to know about the different needles, you should ask them to explain it to you. Or just let them do it if you'd rather not know. That's your choice.

At this step, they also use kits with sterile gloves and a tube attached to the needle where stuff they might flush out can go.

By then, somebody's already put a tall pole next to your chair and, at the top, is a plastic bag full of liquid chemo. The nurse counts one, two, three, and slams the needle into the end of the port's tube. Then they clip it down and tape it in place so you can't yank it out. This works pretty well because then you don't have to get stuck in your arm over and over every day.

So, then the next time I went to the clinic for chemo, my vein was already "accessed," and we kept it that way all week. The length of the actual chemo session varied, anywhere from thirty minutes to three hours depending on what I needed. Finally, I had to wait a little while to make sure there were no bad reactions.

In between chemo treatments, the tube can't get wet. So, they would put another big plastic bandage over it. Then at home, when I needed a shower, Mom would put the end of the tube in another plastic bag and tape the bag to me. I prefer taking tub baths, but with the port, showers were much easier. I wasn't able to go swimming at all.

In my case, chemo and radiation were done together. So, after the chemo, we'd drive fifteen or twenty minutes over to the University of Kansas Cancer Center and have the radiation treatment. (I'll tell you about that in a little bit.) Once we got to the radiation clinic, they would take us in right away, and that treatment only took ten or fifteen minutes.

The whole trip was a big, giant triangle, from Lawrence to Kansas City, then over to the University of Kansas Cancer Center, and then back to Lawrence. By the time we got back home, I'd be pretty exhausted and usually wanted to go to sleep for a while.

About the chemo, there is no feeling, good or bad, to it actually. Usually, you just sit there in the big chair using your phone or computer, or being bored. But it does make you feel something later. It made me sick to my stomach. When I was having the stronger chemo in the hospital, I had to throw up like every thirty minutes. That may sound bad, but it really didn't bother me. I didn't like it, but I got used to it. After a while, it was a struggle gagging and getting it out, but when I finally did it, at least I felt better. Like a small achievement. Even if I didn't have any food in there, throwing up my stomach acids made me feel better.

They call things that are caused or triggered by the chemo *side effects.* You can feel like you have a cold—just sluggish and stuff. But mainly for me, it was feeling like I'd been hit hard—BLAM!—and then just wanting to puke.

I've been asked if I had any hints for kids going through chemo when it gets really bad like that. I would say that if you can't throw up, don't. And if you can eat a little before chemo, that will help give you something to throw up. It shouldn't be a big meal, just like a granola bar or something small. I guess I mean to say that when you haven't got anything in your stomach to throw up, that can sometimes be the worst. And yet, with my new round of chemo, they say don't eat at all before. So, who knows? Different chemicals, different people is all I can say. Ask somebody on your team what would be best for you then.

I've seen nurses give popsicles to little kids getting chemo. Cancer treatments can also *cause cold sores or ulcers in your mouth or on your lips.* Once I had two in the same spot. Maybe because popsicles are wet and cold, they make your mouth feel better. I never tried it. They have medicines that help a lot.

And because you're there for two hours or more, they will usually ask you if you want to order something from the cafeteria. But I found that when I tried eating while getting the chemo, that only made me feel worse. You've got to do what works for you. All I can really say for certain is that for me, when I'm getting chemo, food is the very last thing on my mind!

Other Side Effects

During the very first chemo I took, one of the side effects was something called *chemotherapy-induced peripheral neuropathy* (*CIPN* for short). Basically, it feels like the hot, prickly feeling you get when your foot goes to sleep and then you move it. Only it stays that way all of the time. And when the weather turns cold, it's like sharp pins stabbing you. I have it in my feet; it used to be in my hands and fingers too. Luckily not everybody gets it.

When it happened to me, Dr. Ginn switched up the chemo and gave me some extra medicine so that it wouldn't get any worse. It's helped when it's hot outside, but it hasn't helped in the cold times. It still hurts worse in the cold times. That was four years ago, and I still have it. Dr. Ginn says it could go away in a few more years.

Funny thing is that my dad has neuropathy too. Only he can't feel anything at all. He will take his feet and just bang them on the floor to prove it. I can feel mine.

What I've Learned

Certain types of chemotherapy or radiation can cause peripheral neuropathy. *Peripheral* means the parts at the ends of your body, like your hands and feet. This is a case of the chemo hurting healthy nerve cells at the same time it destroys cancer cells.

Another side effect is that *chemo messes with your taste buds*, so it just feels like you're chewing something. It could be paper or anything because you can't taste it. Maybe that's a good time to eat salad or other healthy stuff that's not delicious. When you are off chemo, you can kind of taste things, but they're never that good. I still can't eat lollipops anymore. It's not that they turn my stomach or anything; I just can't taste them. It's just a useless exercise. Worse, they kind of rip up my tongue now, so no thanks.

About Going Bald

One of the things they tell you right away when you get chemo is that your hair could fall out. Not for everybody, but for a lot of people. And that's what some people immediately think of when they see a kid who's bald. So, I didn't think much about it when they told me. I was pretty naïve in those early days. But the first time you actually *do go bald*, it's a shocker.

What I've Learned

Chemo and radiation attack some fast-growing cancer cells, but sometimes they can damage other fast-growing cells in your body-cells like the ones in your mouth, nose, digestive system, *and* cells in the roots of your hair. So, one way to look at it is that getting sores in your mouth and going bald are just signs that the chemo is working to help you get better.

Sometime in September 2016, I was in the bathtub, washing my hair, and all of a sudden, there was this pile of hair in between my fingers. I mean, everybody has a couple of hairs come out when they wash it, but this was a lot. I mean really a lot. Noticeably. I told Mom about it, but we both just kind of said, "Oh well, we knew this was coming." So, we didn't do anything.

But the next morning, I found a huge clump on my pillow. And that was the real shocker. I think that's when it really hit me.

It's not just the hair on your head. It can be every hair on your body, even your eyelashes, and check the hair on your arms. But, funny thing, I never lost my eyebrows. At least that's how it was with me. Then, the skin that's left itches. The only good thing is that your hair will come back when you take a break from chemo or get to stop it altogether.

Finally, one of the other side effects I've had is that I bruise very easy now. I mean it's like if even a heavy pillow drops on my foot, I'm gonna get a bruise. That's why Dad's nickname for me is Bumpy.

Radiation

Radiation is a treatment that's completely different from chemo. It's faster for one thing. Mainly, it zaps the cancer cells with high-energy electronic waves, like a laser beam directed right to where your tumor is. That means the first thing they have to do is make sure the radiation goes into the exact right spot—every time. So, they give you tattoos for lining up those coordinates. My tumors are in my brain and spine, so to line up the radiation beams, they gave me little tattoos on my chest, one on my pelvis, and one on each side of my body. Getting the tattoos was like getting a lot of little shots. It didn't really hurt much. When I get older, I'm going to have a tattoo around my chemotherapy port.

After the tattoos, they fit you for a helmet—made of white plastic that sort of looks like the full-face mask a hockey goalie wears. It has holes for the eyes and mouth and a lot of little holes or lattice mesh all around.

On the day of the treatment, you go into the clinic, put on your mask, and climb up on a table that's going into a big machine that's a lot like the MRI. They snap together the front and the back of your mask and then attach it to the table with little bolts. All of the technicians then leave and go into a separate room where they can watch you through a window. That may seem weird, like they're getting out of the way of something. But those guys can get exposed to radiation all day every day, and that's not good for them long term. It's not like the little bits you're getting.

Then the big machine goes around and around. It doesn't make too much noise, and there's nothing to be afraid of. It's not going to hurt you or anything. The mask felt a little tight, but I could move up and down. So, the radiation is not like the MRI where I have to stay perfectly still. I can move a little bit, but my mask keeps my head pretty much in one place.

When it's over, you're not radioactive or anything, and sometimes they'll show you pictures of what's inside. Some people get light burns on their skin, but that never happened to me. The main thing it did to me was make me very tired.

Me in the clinic with Theo and my radiation helmet.
You get to ring the bell when you're finished
with your treatment. I still have the helmet.

The Feeding Tube

Like I said before, the chemo and radiation can really mess with how you feel about food. Nothing tastes good, even stuff you love. It's all like chewing cardboard. Or at least, that's how it was for me. And so, I just wasn't hungry. Everybody would try to get me to eat things—all the time: liquid yogurt, Carnation breakfast drinks, sports drinks, and protein shakes, you name it. But nothing tasted good.

Before the cancer, I was kind of a stocky football guy, but after the first round of chemo, I got pretty skinny. In fact, I'd lost about 25–30 percent of my body weight. So, they decided to use a feeding tube. It's just like it sounds, a long, thin plastic tube that they slowly wind up through your nose, until it loops down through the back of your throat into the tunnel-like part of your body called the *esophagus* and then down into your stomach where it can do some good.

Don't be too worried about how they put the tube in because it's all connected in your body—trust me, it's not going to get lost in there because it only has one way to go. Well, there is a second way, and I'll tell you a funny story about that in chapter 5 (page 49).

Anyway, putting the tube in and taking it out is usually pretty easy. Even I could do it by myself after a while.

Well, to be totally honest, the first few times weren't that easy. The nurses always put it in at the hospital, but on the first day we had to put it in after I'd come home, it just so happened that some of my friends from the neighborhood also came over to say hello. My mom was having a hard time getting it in, and the kids thought that was pretty cool. But Mom was starting to fuss about it. I know now it's because she was worried that she couldn't get it in right and we'd have to drive an hour back to the hospital to have somebody there show her how to do it again. Luckily it got easier for everyone in time.

My point is that with all these things in your treatments, you've got to remember that when your parents and your family are trying to do what the nurses showed them, it can take a little trial and error before they get it right. That makes them nervous because they want to do it perfectly. When you can stay calm and relaxed, it really helps them too. Nobody at the hospital is going to ask them to do anything at home that isn't easy once you get the hang of it.

When the tube is in your nose and all the way down to your stomach, you tape it on your face. In my case, we always used the right nostril and taped it to my right cheek to keep it in place. The other end is threaded through a little pump on a stand, and then attached to a plastic bag of liquid food.

The food itself looks kind of like a creamy vanilla breakfast drink. It looked like that, but it sure didn't taste like that; if you put it on your tongue, it tasted nasty. The liquid comes in something like a milk carton, and you have to fill the plastic bag each time. I remember it doesn't have to be refrigerated, which is good, because I don't think I'd like anything cold going down a tube like that.

Once somebody fills the bag, it has a little loop at the end, so it can hang on a pole over your head, like a floor lamp. That way somebody doesn't have to stand there and hold it until it's empty. The little pump slowly moves the food, one drop at a time, and there's a monitor that beeps if the tube gets plugged or when the bag is empty.

Me at our fourth-grade Halloween party.
I went as the Monkey in My Chair. You
can see the feeding tube in my nose.

With the feeding tube, you get all of the nutrients that you need because we're kids and, hungry or not, we're growing all the time. We can't go without food for very long. It's not the greatest thing, and you've got to be the one who decides if you will eat or not. If you're not ready, the feeding tube is a temporary fix. The important thing is that getting food will eventually make you feel better and stronger.

For a few weeks, I had it with me all the time. We could unhook the bag from the pole and put it in a special backpack that I could even wear to school. Turns out your body needs food to fight cancer even if you can't taste much and aren't in the mood for SpaghettiOs or whatever.

My cancer treatments have been going on for a while, and hearing about it gets hard to follow, so I made a list of the main dates and put it all in the back of this book. That way you can get a better idea. The list is located in appendix B (page 125).

Chapter 5
Take Charge
of Pain

Here's the hard thing about talking about pain. First, who even knows what it is? I mean, they know more about *cancer* than they know about pain. Mainly that's because you're the only one who knows what it feels like for you. You can talk about pain; the doctors can talk about pain; everybody talks about it. But they can't feel yours and you can't feel theirs. There's physical pain, and then there's the kind that's even harder to explain because it hurts your feelings. You know, it hits you in the heart. To me the second kind of pain is the hardest to figure out. Maybe it's a guy thing. But I'm not too sure about that.

Let's start with the physical pain that comes when you have cancer. The main point of this book is to tell you everything I wish I'd known before it happened to me. I mean, to me, that's one of the hardest parts—how you can go into it blind. But it's not just a story about agonizing pain. No. Not that. Pain is gonna happen sometimes, yeah, but most of the time, the doctors and nurses are going to give you medicines for that. They show you pictures of the emoji faces, and you pick how bad it is. Then they'll give you medicine if you tell them it hurts more than you can stand. Nobody in the hospital *wants* to hurt you. Or scare you. They will always try to give you medicine to make you numb or not be in pain. That's a lot of what their job is. I've said before that they're not trying to hurt you for no reason. All they want to do is help. So, tell them when you can't take it. Ask them to please go a little slow, and they will. The nurses and the technicians will usually understand and stop to try something different.

What I've Learned

- You want to receive the treatments because they will help make you better.
- In some ways, you can be in charge of your pain and your reaction to what's happening.

There was this one time when I had to take charge, so don't feel bad if you have to do that. I was in the hospital getting a tube put in my nose to go down my throat and into my stomach. And as the technician was putting it in, I could tell that something wasn't right.

So, first, I asked nice, "Can we please take it out? It hurts."

She didn't believe me, and she kept smiling and telling me in this foreign accent, "No, it good. It good."

Well, it wasn't good. I knew something was wrong; it didn't feel like when they'd put in the tube before, and it really hurt with a lot of pressure. I tried telling her, but she still wouldn't listen to me, and she taped the tube on my face like we were all done.

I started coughing and yelling, "Pull it out, pull it out!"

She didn't do anything, and so I barely touched the tube and it just whipped out—all in a big ball. Not with snot or anything, it just whipped out. It hadn't gone down into my stomach after all—it had just curled up in my sinuses—which are these empty places just under your eyes and behind your face. That was funny. I mean, it wasn't fun for me. It was funny because I was right. If an adult, even a doctor, isn't believing what you say you feel—find another one to tell.

What I've Learned

Sinuses are air pockets behind your face and inside your skull. They're located over and under your eyes, and there are little ones under the top of your nose. Mainly they help clean and put moisture in the air you breathe. They also catch a lot of germs and gunk and can get infected and filled up when you have a cold.

Regular Pain

Sometimes pain comes in waves, and you can forget it for a little bit, and during those times, it helps me if I just relax and let it pass over me. Other times, when I feel sick to my stomach and have to throw up—fighting it only makes that go on for longer. You might be different, but if you feel that way too—just go ahead and throw up. Enjoy that a little bit; be happy. Not a "party, party, whoo hoo" kind of a celebration, but a little one.

And when you need to throw up over and over and over and there is nothing left in there, you'll probably get some medicine to make you stop. Then when that feeling goes away, you can get back to what you were doing.

Don't Be Scared Before It Even Happens

Then there's being scared of future pain, and that makes it worse than ever. Take me and needles. When I first started getting stuck with needles, I hated it. I could feel it hurt before they even got close to me. And the more I fought it, the more it hurt.

That's one thing you will have with cancer: lots of people poking needles in you. And it doesn't matter if you like them or not—none of that matters. What matters is that you *have to have them* if you're going to get better. And so, you just have to tell yourself that a needle is what's getting the medicine or the chemo into you so it can do its job. And it's the needle that's getting blood out of you so the doctors can run tests to see if the chemo is working. Or if the cancer is going away, or not.

I remember the worst time when they were testing a new needle at Children's Mercy, and I just happened to be there. Imagine a big, hooked needle with little, almost microscopic spurs on it. Sort of like the barbed wire they put on fences, only a thousand times smaller. This apparently was some sort of fancy experimental needle that was supposed to do its job better than any other needle known to the world. When they put it into the other kids, they were acting like it was sticking a knife into them and then pulling it out. Let me tell you, none of the kids there liked that particular needle. It was just my luck that it seemed like I was the biggest kid there with all these little kids who were just starting their chemo and were really scared. I'd had other needles maybe a hundred times by then, so after a while of watching, I said to the nurses, "Okay, okay. I'll try it." And I made myself sit there to see if I could handle it without yelling or squirming around or anything. I mean, you gotta figure that if you squirm around with that hooked thing, it'd be even worse, right?

I only felt it a little when it was going in, but when they pulled it out, it was like getting caught on a barbed wire fence. It was crazy. It really, *really* hurt. It *was* pretty bad, alright, but of course, I didn't want to scare the little kids even more, so I used all of my concentration to hold still. I didn't scream or anything. I never complained, but later I told the nurses it was like it had prongs on it that were ripping me up when they took it out. So, they knew that if I couldn't take it, no one could!

That's when the nurses started calling me Nick the Brave every time I'd come into the hospital. Like I said before, it wasn't what I ever thought of as being brave. They must've thrown out that experiment because I never got the barbed needle again.

Funny thing was, after that, I kind of got used to it when a normal needle was being stuck in. Sometimes they have these wipes with novocaine or one of those others, and you won't feel a thing.

When You Just Get Tired of It

If you feel like taking a nap, take it. And it helps to get into regular sleep patterns at night, going to bed and waking up on the same schedule. Mom helps me do that. Going to sleep isn't that easy for me, and sometimes I have to take melatonin pills—two or three at a time, depending.

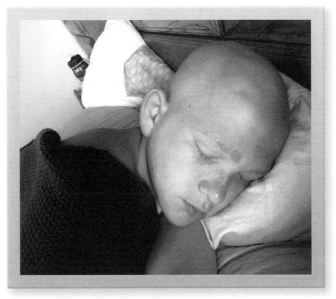

Me, sleeping or thinking, or maybe both.

That's when you can really think about things as the medicine is getting to work. Your mind is the most powerful thing you've got. So, you should use it. Somebody told me once that if you didn't use your brain, you might as well have feet on both ends. That means taking charge. Sometimes you can tell yourself to relax, really listen, and you can do it. Give it a try. I'm not saying you can always make the pain totally go away, but you can get used to it, or make it calm down a little. Your mind is more powerful than you know.

For me, that works best with the little pains like how my joints feel, especially in the cold. I feel old because all my joints hurt, and I get pain in my feet a lot. I like the wintertime, and it's my favorite season, but when it gets cold, my joints hurt worse. That's just how it is.

What I've Learned
Half of all the bones in your body are in your feet and hands. There are twenty-eight bones and thirty-three joints in each foot and ankle.

Sleeping can make it feel better, but, of course, you can't sleep all day every day. So, other times focus on the things that make you feel good. A game or texting with your friends or listening to your favorite music. Or just let yourself go! Once, I had just come home from a chemo round. Usually, after that, as the chemo is soaking in, you just feel like all you want to do is go to bed. But that day for some reason, I ran out into the yard and just yelled and shouted as loud as I could, "Yay, I just did a whole round of chemo!" It was a celebration because I was proud that I'd done it. And happy it was over.

But what I didn't know was that one of our neighbors, this guy who used to get balls out of the trees when we played kickball, was out in his yard. Well, I must have scared him to death, because he ran over all shocked and excited to see what was wrong. I was a little embarrassed to have made such a big deal and get him worried, but it *was* pretty funny. And it actually made my day to know there are still a lot of good people in the world.

Lots of times when I'm not feeling good, I watch a movie to take my mind off of things. I like horror movies, especially the old ones like *The Shining*, which aren't that scary by today's standards. Some of my other favorites are *The Green Mile*, *Forrest Gump*, and *Titanic*. I love how Forrest Gump shows the bullies how fast he can run, and my favorite line is when he says, "Jenny and me was like peas and carrots." One thing does bother me about *Titanic* though—I mean, she could've moved over—that piece of paneling was big enough for him to get on and be saved too. Most of my friends don't like watching old movies like I do. But that doesn't bother me. Whatever helps take your mind off of feeling bad is worth it. If you don't like old movies, read or do something—whatever you like. See your friends, pet one of your critters, or just look at the sky.

Sometimes just taking a shower and putting on my favorite old clothes like my gray sweatpants and a sweatshirt makes me feel better. Look for those things, and ask the people around you to help you if you need it.

I'm not saying you can just make the pain go away by wishing about it. No, nothing like that. It isn't a simple wish. If that were true, we wouldn't even be talking about it. But in some ways, you can get used to it.

The Hardest Kind of Pain

The hardest kind of pain comes from how people can treat you when they don't understand or are scared themselves. Sometimes you might even get bullied.

Let me say right now, if you're a bully or you've ever been bullied, this is the time to stop. You should be done with that now. You've got a more important job, and that's fighting cancer. You might ask, What does that have to do with cancer? To me, learning how to fight bullies is a lot like learning to fight the cancer. Not fight like punching, but you'll see what I mean.

I was bullied in the daycare after second grade. I hate when adults in charge let bullying take place. And that's what happened here because it was her son who was the bully. He was in my group, and when he'd be getting ready for football practice, he would step on my legs with his football cleats. I tried to tell his mom, but she said, "He wouldn't do that." There's always something, because lots of times bullies don't get in trouble. Things in life aren't always fair. For me, that time, it only stopped when we went to another daycare.

There are a few things I'd like to say right off about bullies.

The last thing you want to do is give them the power. You need to take control, and sometimes that can be to walk away, and sometimes that can be to hit them with a verbal zinger. More about that later.

Believe it or not, many of them are more scared of you than you might be of them. They act big and mean because they are scared.

For me personally, I get mad when I see somebody bullying somebody else. And so, I think it's okay if you want to step in and stand up for the person being bullied. For example, you can say, "Just stop it," or, "You don't know what you're talking about."

If you want to. Only if you want to. Otherwise, like I said, just walk away and concentrate on other things.

The older I get, the more kids my age get more attitude. And maybe it's because just going through cancer seems so much bigger to me than anything else bad, that the stupid kids with attitude seem so immature. I mean, "Haven't you got anything better to do?" I want to say.

I'm not talking about the normal kind of things friends do with each other. Like my brother says, you can insult your friends because you know that that's not a real attack. My brother's friends insult each other, and me too sometimes. But anybody else, no. The people I don't really hang out with, no. They haven't got that right. But I don't know; you may have a different idea about that.

I think the only time I ever felt good about beating a bully happened about a year ago when I burned a guy who was making fun of me at school. That's one time when I really felt like I had the power. It was just over some stupid thing I couldn't do—I can't even remember what now. But anyway, he was making fun of me.

I remember he said something like, "Well, what *can* you do then?"

And I said, "Well, I beat cancer twice. Now shut up!"

My brother thought that was pretty good. He was proud of me for doing it because I stood up for myself, and I've used it a couple of times since.

Maybe what's worse is when strangers stare at you when you're out in public. If they do it once, it can be okay because they don't know what to think or they've never seen a kid with cancer before. But when they stare at you more than twice, that's when you have to make a decision about how you're going to handle it. You can walk away, or you can say something.

Like, when I was a little kid, I happened to like a character from the movie *Toy Story* who was named Lotso. He was a big pink bear and a villain who talked with a Southern accent and smelled like strawberries. He had some bad things happen to him before and that made him so sad that he turned into a bully. For most of the story, he's not a very good guy, but I always thought it might be because people weren't listening to how sad he really was.

Later, when I was maybe a little too old for the story, we went to Disneyland, and Mom bought me this great pink Lotso hat because mothers remember what you like. First, let me say that boys get judged sometimes when they wear pink. And that seems really stupid to me. I mean, it's just a color, right? And anyway, I was kind of a Disney nerd then, and I'd had a lot of good memories of Lotso when I was a kid. So, I loved this hat. I mean, I really loved it.

It had been a fun day, but my neuropathy was making it hard for me to walk, and I was getting tired; so, we went to the bus station where they have colored buses to take you back to your hotel. They make it very easy—your hotel has the blue bus, or the yellow bus, and you get on that one with no worries that you'll make it back to the hotel okay.

And there was a kid right near where Mom and I sat down. But out of the corner of my eye, I could see that he was staring at me. Okay, at the time, I was older than the average Lotso fan—and bald. I get it. But when I looked at him, he gave me this bad look—like, "I'm not looking at you. What are you looking at?" Then he turned away. In other words, he knew that I saw him staring at me even though he was trying to pretend that he wasn't. I went back to talking with Mom, but then he did it again! He stared at me, and when I looked at him, he turned away and pretended he didn't.

That's when you get annoyed and stuff. So now, let me say to everybody, when you're looking at someone with cancer or a cancer survivor and they have spots in their hair that you can see through to their scalp, don't be looking at them weird and making them feel bad.

Even some adults are going to stare at you like that when they should be respectful and teach their kids to be respectful too. I'm okay with the little kids like under five looking at me. It's fine. But when you're a twelve-year-old and at Disneyland, staring at another kid your age because he has no hair and is wearing a pink Lotso hat, you should know better. I'm fine with them asking, but I'm not okay with them staring at me or anybody that has cancer. It's mean.

I'm bringing this up because I want you to know that these things are going to happen. And when they do, you should remember that a bald head is beautiful—or in my case, handsome. I want you to know that you have that power. I'm not saying that you should brag about being bald, but you should remember that you're just as beautiful or as handsome as anybody else.

When you get into these situations and if you want to say something, you can. It's up to you. But you also don't have to bother.

With this kid who was apparently bothered by me, I said to myself, "If you want to ask a question, *ask a question*. Ask me *why* I'm bald and why I'm wearing a big, pink hat. That's fine, we can talk about it. But just don't stare and then turn away like you didn't."

Another time, there was this kid who was acting up on the last day of school. We were all signing each other's yearbooks, and he took a red pen and carved his name into the arm of a friend of mine. It really hurt her when he did that. I just hated that behavior. And why I was so upset and sure about that is because he did it to the nicest girl I've ever met in my life.

I ask you, Who does something like that on the last day of school? Who makes trouble on the last day of school? I mean, it wasn't like the teachers couldn't find out who hurt her—I mean, who do you think did it? His name was right there in red ink!

I think that just proves that lots of times bullies are just idiots. If somebody stares or makes fun of you, let me say now that you should stand up for yourself. If they just have a polite question, of course, you should explain that you have cancer and it's the chemo that made your hair fall out and it will all come back when you're better. These people are not really saying that you look like a monster—they just don't know the whole story. And if they don't like it, who cares? It's just their opinion; yours is just as good.

The whole point is to just be honest with people. If you don't like it, you don't have to do it. And to everyone else, if you don't understand why kids with cancer are bald, just ask.

Probably the worst time I ever felt bad in my heart didn't have to do with a bully or with somebody staring at me. It had to do with a doctor's visit. Now, I've told you that doctors only want to help you, and that's true. But some of them are not as good as the others in how they go about it. And this particular time happened because of what people call "going through puberty."

What I've Learned

Puberty is when your body grows and changes from being a little kid to first being a teenager and then being an adult. It happens when hormones (some of the regular chemicals in your body) send messages to your brain, blood, tissues, and other body parts telling them what to do. Hormones are like a trigger.

The whole thing can take years, and exactly *when* you go through puberty is totally up to the individual. It happens when your own, individual body says it's time to happen. That's because your body is different depending on your hormones, how old other people in your family were when they went through puberty, and your general health. Even horrible things like living in a war zone can make a difference. So, it makes sense that some cancers and some chemo treatments that kids get can cause puberty to come early or come late. And there was a time when the doctors thought that my cancer or the chemo could be affecting me. I must have been eleven or twelve; I can't remember Anyway, we went to a hormone doctor to see what was happening. I was really interested in talking to this special doctor, because when I'm older, I want to have kids of my own someday. That's what I want.

What I've Learned

A doctor who specializes in your glands and hormones is called an *endocrinologist*.

Well, this guy told me that I couldn't have kids. Never. Now, I mean, who says that to a twelve-year-old kid! I've since learned that I can; it's just going to be hard to. Science is always finding out new ways, and I've got plenty of years for that to happen. I still like most doctors, just not that one. He wasn't very thoughtful, and he sure shouldn't have been talking to kids.

Looking back, I would have to say that's the bravest thing I've ever done. Because at the time, sitting in his office, I really wanted to just bawl my eyes out. But I didn't. I didn't want him to think he could make me cry.

Chapter 6
You're Not Alone

When you have cancer—your family is going to mean just about everything. All families are different. Some are big; some are small. Loud or quiet. Whatever. Family. What you've got you've got! They will be the ones who are always looking out for you. The ones you can count on. At least, that's been how it's been for me. I've learned that everybody who lives at your house is called your *immediate* family, but other family living anywhere can be grandparents, aunts, uncles, cousins, neighbors, or old friends of your parents who've just been around forever. My dad's side has a lot of that kind. I'm pretty lucky to have a big family on my team.

Me (back when I was a real little kid) and my big brother, David, taking in the sights from the Top of the Rock in NYC. David is always there for me.

Once during the first year I had cancer, my aunt Marillyn and uncle Mark put together a "poker run" to help raise money for my treatments. It's this big event that's a cross between a card game and a race with a bunch of four-wheelers and motorcycles that have to drive a designated route. Along the way are four stops, where you eat, party, and draw a playing card. Then the last card is back at the starting point, and the goal is to see who got the best hand of poker. That meant they won a prize. They also had an auction with a lot of different prizes—and black tee shirts and sweatshirts with gold letters that said, "Wear gold for the cute bald kid." That was me, of course. We really had a lot of fun that day.

Friendships and Keeping in Touch Under the Circumstances

Even though I go to a Catholic school now, I still have a great group of friends from my old public school. And I'm especially glad that all my friends and their parents treat me like a regular kid. No different than anybody else. Like when I go visit my friend Trevor, his mom treats me pretty much like part of the family. And the same for him when he comes to my house.

As I told you, I was just going into the fourth grade when we first learned I had cancer. And my friends at that school were okay about it. They didn't baby me or do things everybody needs to do for themselves. And when I got so thin and had to come to school with my feeding tube stuck up my nose and down into my stomach, that was no big deal. My teacher that year was Mrs. ML, and I liked her very much. Her last name was really Miescher-Lerner, but she said we could call her Mrs. ML.

She always told the other kids about it when I had to go away, and we even had some time when we could talk about it a little and they could ask me questions. That's when they'd use the Monkey in My Chair.

Little Theo, Me, and Big Theo for
my chair in Mrs. ML's class.

There was one funny thing that happened in that class when I was first getting chemo. We were taking a math test, and all of a sudden, when I rubbed my head to think, my hair started falling out all over the desk. I know kids around me noticed, and it must have been a shock to them, but nobody said anything. Finally, I got up and asked Mrs. ML if I could go to the nurse. I mean, there I was, holding clumps of hair in my hand. She handled it pretty well, and like I said, it was kind of funny thinking about it later. Best of all, I didn't have to finish the test.

One of the main reasons I switched out of the public school when I got to junior high is because you have to meet certain gym requirements that I was having trouble with. Like when I got really sick, I couldn't even do a simple jumping jack. We'd done that a lot when I was in football, but this time I couldn't even come close. My feet were affected by the chemo (that's the neuropathy I talked about earlier), and my muscles everywhere were too. So, it didn't do any good to try. That's how much cancer and the treatments can take out of you. You've got to accept that for a while at least—you can't do the physical things you once could do. You don't have the energy, or you might feel like you're going to throw up for long periods of time. It's like when I got a new bike, and I couldn't ride it like before. Yes, you've got to stay positive—I said that, and I meant it. But if you can't do something, you can't. Live with it!

Worst of all, that teacher just kept yelling at me to keep trying. When I got home and told Mom and Dad about it, we decided I could go to Corpus Christi, the Catholic school in our parish. I really like the new school and will probably go there through the eighth grade.

I've gotta admit I'm not looking forward to then going to public high school the year after. I'll like that I'll be closer to being a doctor, but I'm not looking forward to it because I've heard that the kids get a lot more attitude during that time—meaner. We'll see. I might be surprised. We don't have a Catholic high school in Lawrence, and the closest one is about twenty-five miles away in Topeka. My friend Trevor will probably go to that school next year, and my friend Braden will probably go to public high school with me. We'll see; it's still up in the air.

What I've Learned

Being a good friend means:

- Being nice and caring, even when you're having a bad day.
- Not just listening when they talk, but really paying attention.
- Sharing or helping them out when you can.

> o If they tell you a secret, they can trust that you're not going to blab to everybody*.
>
> *There is an exception to that last one. If the secret is about somebody getting hurt, you should tell your parents or the teacher-but you should also let your friend know up front that has to happen.

I really like sharing with my friends when it can work out that way. Last year, Sporting Kansas City (shortened to Sporting KC), a professional soccer team in Kansas City, had an event for kids who had relapsed back into cancer. It was a whole weekend, and best of all, each kid got to bring two friends. I took my friends Trevor and Chase. I am not a soccer guy, and so I may not have even gone myself, but Trevor and Chase both play, so I was really happy that I could share something I knew they were going to like.

First, Sporting KC gave us tickets to a soccer match where we all got to sit in special seats. They announced us cancer kids before the national anthem and put our pictures up on the jumbotron. Then the crowd gave us a big chant, "You got this! You got this!" That was exciting.

We all got shirts and these big team scarves. Then the cancer kids got to go out on the field with the players, and after the match, they signed soccer balls for us

We also got two days at a recreation park called Great Wolf Lodge where we went on a scavenger hunt. I'd been there before when I was younger, and it's a really nice place for younger kids. We were just a little too old for it, but we had a great time together anyway. Acting silly. Nothing bad, just silly. Like we didn't have to impress anybody, so we relaxed and had fun. I felt great about sharing with my two friends because they have both given me so much.

Me, Trevor, and Chase sharing the soccer
match thanks to Sporting KC.

Now that everybody has to stay separated because of COVID-19, I really like playing online games like Fortnite and Minecraft with my friends. And when we can get together, my favorite is playing a game with Trevor, called Oculus Quest—it's a virtual reality headset, which can be a challenge for people who have glasses.

I have glasses, but I don't wear them a lot. I tried contacts, but they just didn't work for me. When they're trying to see if you want contacts, they ask if you can touch your eye. I can touch my eye alright, but I can't put the contacts in by myself. So, I can get them in at the eye doctor's, but once I take them home, it's useless. I can see pretty good without my glasses if something's nearby. But if it's far away, I can't really see it clearly. Using the Oculus Quest without my glasses works for me.

What I've Learned

When you can see things close up without glasses, but things far away are not so clear, that's called nearsightedness. That's what I've got. When, without glasses, you can see things farther away better than you can see things close up, that's called farsightedness.

Anyway, when Trevor and I play Oculus, our favorite game is called Robo Recall where we shoot robots. When you're in the game, your enemy is like a company of robots that have gone rogue. They've turned on their human creators and started killing them. So, you have to get them first. Not all of the time, but sometimes when I really get into it, I can imagine they're like cancer cells. Your character can have an official sounding name like Agent 34, and you have two pistols that you can use. There are lots of expensive gaming add-ons, but Trevor and I have enough fun with the basic set.

I like looking into the future. These headsets are so cool. You can play the game and think about what could be true someday. That's an important point, I think, when you're thinking about living your life with cancer. So, for me, imagining the future is a break and a place to relax.

Special Friends

It's important to have special friends you can talk to. Like, when I was going through my chemotherapy trial, Hailey, one of my special friends, asked me what it was like. And when I told her, she started crying. That showed me she really got it; she understood. I didn't have to explain anything more.

Now—to anyone reading this who doesn't have cancer, you don't have to cry when people tell you about tough times, but if you can show them that you're paying attention and that you're concerned about them, that can mean a lot to someone. Sometimes it can be as simple as just asking them if they want to say anything else.

When you work on special friendships, people will show you parts of their personalities that they don't always express to anybody else.

You get to see them when they're vibrant and when they're more comfortable. And in the same way, you can relax and not feel that you have to be guarded or fake around them. You don't have to worry about what you're saying. If you fall off your bike, do something stupid, or look silly, they're not going to spread it around to the whole school. That's like me and Hailey. And me and Trevor and Chase, too. We know we can trust each other.

Hailey and Me at the Drop Tower in Worlds of Fun amusement park, Kansas City. I loved this! Hailey said it was okay.

Going Back to School and It's All Changed!

I wasn't able to go to school for two years when the chemo rounds were at their strongest, and people have said to me, "You must be happy now to be back in school." I'll tell you a secret. In my own mind, the answer is, "Yes, but only sometimes." I do want to be an oncologist, and, of course, I know that takes lots and lots of schooling. So, I do try to stay interested in it.

Of course, this COVID-19 thing has really messed up a lot. When you're taking chemo, your immune system is down—weaker than normal—and you're more likely to catch whatever's going around. COVID-19 and illnesses like it are too much of a risk for us cancer kids. I hear that they've got a vaccine for it now, and I think five years from now we'll all be talking about COVID-19 just like it's the common cold.

What I've Learned

A vaccine is a tiny, harmless bit of a bad virus. It teaches your body's immune system how to fight harder, which is how you get over it.

At my school, they started with remote learning after Labor Day in 2020 with the hopes of opening up after the first semester.

We talked to Dr. Ginn about whether or not I should go if they did open, and he shook his head and said, "I wouldn't. There are too many unknowns at this point, so let's just not push it."

After that, Mom and Dad set up a homeschool office for me, with some new desks and the computer, so I can concentrate. And my podcasts and YouTube program can be my independent learning projects. Actually, writing this book is an independent project too.

Virtual schooling makes it easier to catch up, I guess. Still, after being out for two years, it's very overwhelming how much work I have in the eighth grade. I'm studying math, pre-algebra, American history, and English.

Mostly in the virtual schooling, they just give you assignments. Read this, then write something on it. I have to read chapters of Harry Potter every day now. I like Harry Potter; I can watch it fine at the movies, but I'm kind of lukewarm when it comes to reading about him. The worst part has to be that you don't get to see the teachers like in a video chat or Zoom; you only read the emails from them.

My favorite subject is American history. One of the things I don't understand is why we bounce around in the book, reading some of this then something else at a completely different time. I don't understand why we don't use the whole book start to finish. That's how history works, right? Maybe they have a reason for doing that, but I haven't figured it out yet.

I don't like math that much, but I know I have to study it in order to be a doctor. My other classmates did pre-algebra in seventh grade, but since I couldn't go to school then, I have a tutor now and I'm catching up. His name is also Nicholas, and he lives in Washington, DC. I'm good at math in some ways, but not so good at it in other ways. It takes a lot of practice, but once you get math, it's like a game and pretty fun. I was supposed to practice math yesterday, but I flaked out to go over to my friend's house—just because. I also talk to the tutor about drawing and art, which he likes too. He knows a lot about art.

Falling behind in a subject or two can happen when you need to take time off to fight your cancer. But don't worry about it—you *can* catch up. Lots of kids do that all of the time. Lucky for me, so many of my friends are smart in math, so they can help too. Like my friend, Chase, whose dad, just as a coincidence, was one of my dad's fraternity brothers. Chase is like a human calculator.

I'm pretty much a people person, so I don't like that we can't be with any of the other students. I'll be happy when we can get back to normal, and I think there are a lot of things we don't study in school that we should.

Learning to Deal With How People See You

Dealing with strangers and people you barely know is similar to what Father Mick once told Mom about how you have to "lean in" to new things. You've got to understand where people are coming from while still standing up for yourself.

First, nobody you meet really can do much or wave a magic wand or anything to take the cancer away. Even your doctors and your family can't always do that as much as they want to. But most people have good hearts. They want to help in some way, but don't know how. Once, the first time I relapsed and had to go back for another round of chemo, I was at my friend's house telling him all about it. One of his neighbor's overheard us. He just walked over to me and said, "You just did a round of chemo? Well, let me shake your hand, son." And then he did. It just made my day.

Understanding that is what I think it means to lean in. And that usually makes everybody feel better. Besides, you will get some funny or weird experiences—like I find it so weird that so many people want to rub my bald head!

The first few times somebody wanted to rub my head, it was a real shocker. But no harm done. And it felt okay. I just couldn't see what the big deal was. I figured that when I first had chemo, I was still pretty young—and being bald, I must have looked like a baby. I know adults like touching babies—I mean can you imagine what a baby has to put up with? So early on, I would say to myself, "Okay, you can do it. I'll put up with it. Just do it!"

Then later, I'll admit it got a little annoying, and I would want to say, "What's going on? Are you crazy? I don't even know you!" But I never did say that out loud.

Finally, and you may come to this point, depending on the type of chemo you have and your reaction to it, your head can get pretty sore. Your scalp can burn or itch! That's when, if people asked, I started telling them, "No," but in a nice way. You will want to be ready to make that decision too if the time comes.

I'll have to say that the funniest head-rubbing experience happened was once when my dad and I stopped at a big convenience store with a gas station. Sometimes when he can be there to watch, he'll let me put the nozzle in the car and fill up the tank. So, we were doing that when a woman, a total stranger, came over to us and asked my dad if she could pray for me. I guess she figured out I had cancer because I was bald and everything.

Dad turned to me and said, "What do you think, Bumpy?" (Again, that's his nickname for me.)

And I said, "Sure, why not?"

Imagine how shocked we both were when she suddenly put her hand on the top of my head, spread out her fingers to kind of grab me, and started yelling to God. And the yelling got louder and louder.

"Lord. Remove the devil out of this boy!" she shouted. "Remove the devil inside!! Remove him, Lord!!!"

Then she took her hand away, turned, and walked away to her car.

Dad and I were both shocked for a few seconds, and then we just started laughing. I was fine. So, we went into the store and bought our stuff and paid for the gas. It didn't hurt anything, but it was also pretty weird. Everybody has a right to their own religion and that was part of hers, I guess.

Now that I'm older, it doesn't happen as much. And if it does, I usually just decide to laugh it off. If it makes them feel better somehow, that's fine with me.

Of course, even I can see that *this* is a rub-able head.

Chapter 7
Special Opportunities

Father Mick once told my mom that sometimes you've got to let people do things for you. You have to let them. Because it's just as important for them to be able to help as it is for you to have it done. He calls it "leaning in." Even if you're embarrassed, because you think it's like charity or something. It isn't charity. No.

When people see a kid with cancer, they feel horrible. They wish they could do something. And they can't. Well, they *can't*, and they *can*. That's the funny part. It can be both. And you don't always know which until later.

So, when somebody wants to give you a toy or cool experience, just say thank you and appreciate that they wanted to help. Even if it's something you think you don't need, you can still put it to good use—you can pass it on to some other kid who really does need it. Or, you never know, you might find out later that it works for you and you can't be without it. The point is it's a good and positive thing they're doing, and as you know, I only surround myself with positive things.

This first made sense to me when I was in sixth grade. I had just changed from public school to the parochial school, Corpus Christi. It was probably the year that I felt the most sick. I had lost so much weight; I was tired of being sick; and I was the new kid. The new, "bald kid." It was a low point. I didn't feel like a big, tough-looking guy anymore. On top of that, the school I was going to was pretty hard. Mom calls it rigor; I just thought we had way too much to do. I had a ton of books.

Some of the other parents went to Father Mick and said they wanted to buy me an expensive rolling backpack. The best rolling backpack they could find. Anonymously. They didn't want me to know who they were; they didn't want any credit; they just wanted to help me out. But I already had a perfectly good backpack. It wasn't fancy, but it was okay. And I said, "No, I didn't want it."

Then I could hear Father Mick saying, "Remember—let people do things for you. Lean in."

So, I changed my mind and said yes. That was two years ago. I still have that pack, and when I need it, it does come in handy. Now, even though I never got to thank them in person—and I don't even know who they are—I feel good about them every time I use it. Father Mick said it makes them feel good too.

The Big Slick

It may sound weird to say that cancer can bring anything like an opportunity, but it does. One kind of opportunity you will get happens with fundraisers put together by people in your town. Usually, it will be the social worker on your team at the hospital who can introduce you to these events.

My first experience with a big fundraiser was in June of 2017. The Big Slick is a fundraiser for Children's Mercy, and it raises a ton of money for kids with cancer. The hospital uses the money for research, equipment, and other special things for the kids. It was started by five celebrities who all grew up in the Kansas City area: Paul Rudd (he was in *Ant-Man* and in lots of other movies), Jason

Sudeikis (he was on *Saturday Night Live*), Eric Stonestreet (he is Cameron from *Modern Family*), David Koechner (he plays Murray's best friend on *The Goldbergs*), and Rob Riggle (he was in movies too and *The Daily Show*, but mainly he was a Marine like my dad).

The Big Slick is held over a weekend, and on Friday night, everybody goes to a celebrity softball game before the Kansas City Royals play their regular game. Mom bought us tickets to the locker room and dugout because she wanted us to do our part to contribute to the hospital. We also got to meet all the celebrities.

The next day some of us kids got to play bocce ball with the founders, and we ran into a group of people, called donors, from the night before.

What I've Learned

Donors give out of their own pockets to fundraisers that help kids with things like cancer. Since it was started, the Big Slick has raised over eight million dollars for Children's Mercy Hospital. And that's just one event in our one hometown.

When you participate in these things, you feel good not only because you meet other kids who are fighting and winning against cancer, but also because you see how many people are working to help you get better. And it lasts beyond the event. For example, we became good friends with a woman named Kerri Sitrin and her husband, Henry. Kerri wrote a nice thing about me in one of her online posts, and they still keep in touch with us. Jedd and Dara Canty are donors to the Big Slick, and they also have become friends of our family. Not too long ago, my friends from the Big Slick even gave me a big LEGO set for a blue Bugatti sports car. I'm building that with my friends Trevor and Juaquin.

Me and another kid talking to Paul Rudd.

Me and Paul Rudd at The Big Slick, 2017.

Make-A-Wish® Foundation

Around May of 2018, about two years after the diagnosis, we thought the chemo and radiation had done their jobs. That the monster was dead. But it came back. A relapse.

What I've Learned

You know how chemo and radiation are supposed to search out and kill cancer cells? Well, sometimes they don't all get caught. It's like they escape from the main group and hide, too small to be detected. Then, when you think it's all over, they spring back up again, meaner than ever. That's called a *recurrence* or a *relapse*.

So, there I was back in the hospital at Children's Mercy. That's when one of the care assistants or therapists came in and told me about Make-A-Wish. This is a program where kids with critical illnesses get one wish. And you can't be one of those people who says, "I wish for a million Make-A-Wishes." No, you can't be like that.

So, I said to her, "Can you wish for two wishes?"

"No," she said, "You couldn't. No."

So, then I asked, "If you get cancer again, if you relapse, can you get another wish then?"

And she said that, no, you can't do another one. One per person, like forever.

So, I told her that I needed to think about it.

I thought of all these famous people I'd love to meet, like Dwayne "The Rock" Johnson; he's an actor, who used to be a football player and a wrestler. He was in *The Fast and the Furious*, *Jumanji*, all those shows. Then I thought of this YouTuber I really like.

But Mom said, "No. Don't waste a chance like this on a YouTuber you don't know anything about or have any connection to." And that made sense.

After considering a lot of other people, I thought that, for most of them, I wouldn't have much that we could do together—we'd just take a lot of pictures and stuff. So, then I thought of meeting Chef Gordon Ramsay because I'd watched him all my life.

My dad likes cooking, and before he got into sales, he used to work in a restaurant with my uncle Randy. He tells me stories about what that was like. How to cook and stuff. I really like cooking, and I understand it because it's all about putting together the right ingredients, with the right temperatures, at the right times. You have to do things right for it all to work. And I like being with Dad.

My favorite thing to cook is shrimp Alfredo, and I'm always up for baking, where you have to be more accurate with everything. No mess ups, or it's ruined. Flat! Just like that!

We like to watch *MasterChef* and *MasterChef Junior*. We don't watch *Hell's Kitchen* anymore because there's too much cussing. Chef Ramsay is nice on *MasterChef* and only yells when the food is horrible. On *Hell's Kitchen*, he has to yell more because some of those guys are just a bunch of smokers who complain a lot. But they're always grateful when they figure out that he's right.

So, on my Make-A-Wish application, we put that I wished I could meet Chef Gordon Ramsay. And we turned it in.

One day, when I wasn't even thinking about it, he called me from London, England! I remember exactly what he said at the end of the call, "We'll do it then, mate!"

We were going to meet him on his next business trip to Hollywood. Everybody got to come, Mom, Dad, and my brother, David. And we even got a credit card for spending money. Make-A-Wish picked up the whole tab.

I was excited about flying out to Hollywood, because I'd never been before. And if you want to know my first impression—I liked it. Everything but the traffic, that is, which is very, very slow.

When we got to the hotel, we went outside to the Walk of Fame, which is where famous people in show business have a big metal star with their name and stuff on it, and it's planted in the middle of the sidewalk. People go crazy over those stars. They lean down and get their pictures taken with the metal star, and they leave flowers and notes as if the real star will come by and pick them up, which I don't think really ever happens. And we also went to the Hollywood Wax Museum, which has a bunch of statues of famous people, but I didn't recognize many of them.

Finally, it was time to meet Chef Ramsay.

We went to the GIPHY Studios, where they make GIFs. And for those of you who've seen them but didn't know what they are called, they're those little action video clips you can add to text messages or emails.

I remember being totally shocked when I saw him. It was like a character from a video game coming to life. I could barely talk, but I think I said, "You're really here!"

We were both polite at first and said things like, "Nice to meet you."

Then we talked for a while about our trips there; like, he had flown over all the way from his home in London to Hollywood, and I was coming from Kansas for the first time. I didn't ask if he'd ever been to Kansas, and he didn't say. Then we took some videos. He was very nice and made me feel like we could be *mates* (which is what they call friends in England).

We filmed a GIF that was a takeoff on something from an episode of *Hell's Kitchen*, where he takes two pieces of bread and holds them up to the sides of this woman's head and yells, "What are you?!"

And she yells back, "I'm an idiot sandwich!"

We did it to each other. And it was funny.

The thing that surprised me the most was that he didn't cuss a lot. He did it once, and then he told me that cussing is bad, and so I shouldn't do it.

I told him I didn't want to be a cook when I grow up. I like to cook, but I want to be an oncologist. And he said that was okay. I told him I had four dogs and two cats, and he has about that many too.

His daughter Matilda is around my age, and she has a show in England about their family and cooking. I've seen it a couple of times, and it's pretty good. Before he left, he gave me one of her cookbooks that she'd signed and one of his cookbooks that he'd signed, and he signed my dad's copy of his book, which I'd brought with me. My family really likes books.

Make-A-Wish also gave us tickets for Universal Studios, where we spent a lot of time at the Harry Potter exhibit. Then back at the hotel, we went swimming in the rooftop pool, where I met a woman who produces rapper videos.

We were there for five days and had a great time! The whole trip went like a snap of the fingers. Chef Ramsay was a really terrific guy. I like thinking about meeting him when I cook with Dad, and we go over the trip and laugh again about being an idiot sandwich.

Me and Chef Gordon Ramsay in Hollywood.

Super Bowl LIV

In January of 2020, we really thought the cancer was gone, and I hadn't had any treatments for three months. Then we got the bad news that I'd had another relapse. The cancer monster had come back, meaner and uglier than ever. Dr. Ginn, my oncologist, suggested a different kind of treatment, this time a cancer trial.

What I've Learned

A cancer trial is when you're put in a study being conducted by the hospital, a drug company, or a university. In the study, they will be trying to find out if one type of medicine or treatment works better than other things they've tried before. You get a chance to have the latest and greatest stuff they know about, but most important-you're helping them learn how to make other kids with cancer get better in the future.

About that time, one of the people we met at the first Big Slick, a guy named Nick Paradise, called Mom to say that he had a friend living in Miami, Florida, who had a neighbor named Mark Evans. Mark is a motivational speaker, sales coach, author, and entrepreneur, and he gives a lot of things to help people. One of the things he wanted to give away was a trip to the Super Bowl LIV game between the San Francisco 49ers and my favorite football team of all time, the Kansas City Chiefs. Nick told my mom that he had nominated me.

Naturally, when I heard about the chance for the tickets and the trip, I told Mom we had to go for it. She helped me make a video clip where I told him all about my cancer, why I loved football, and why I just had to see that game in person. I showed him my lucky shoes and my Kansas City Chiefs cap, and I was wearing my Kansas City sweatshirt. Then I kind of forgot about it.

I think the point I want to make here is that you can't let having cancer stop you from dreaming big. Because sometimes dreams do come true. There I was, going into my third round of chemo—fortunately, this time with a new oral medication from the trial instead of the port—when we got a phone call from Mark Evans, who was announcing the winner of the Super Bowl trip live on Facebook.

He talked to Mom for a minute, and then he asked to speak to me. I didn't know what to think.

All I remember him saying was, "My man, you're goin'."

I couldn't believe it! I had won that trip! To the Super Bowl!! I actually yelled and threw the phone in the air; I was so excited.

And before I knew it, we were on our way to the biggest game of my lifetime. The Friday night before the game, Mom and I were in first-class plane seats flying from Kansas City to Miami, and then we went straight to a fancy hotel called the Margaritaville Hollywood Beach Resort.

The next morning, Saturday, February 1, Mark came to give us the game tickets (which Mom and Dad had framed and are still hanging on our wall).

Me and Mark at the Margaritaville Hollywood
Beach Resort. I've been to two completely different
Hollywoods—one in California and one in Florida.

After the meeting, we had time to ourselves to explore around the hotel, but mainly I remember just sleeping most of the day in that giant hotel bed. It was wonderful.

Game day was Sunday, February 2, 2020. One of the last things like that we could do before COVID-19 shut everything down.

But I had no idea it was going to turn into such an historic trip.

Of course, we went early because Mom said she wanted me to experience as much as possible. We got there at about 1 p.m. to watch the stadium fill up, see what was happening pre-game on the sidelines, and generally feel the excitement of the event. Best of all, we beat the real crowds. We got into the souvenir shop before it filled up. That would have been impossible later. We got our food before the lines got really big. And then we saw Troy Aikman, who used to be the quarterback for the Dallas Cowboys. Mom was pretty excited about that.

Then, Maxwell "Bunchie" Young walked right past us. Bunchie is around my age and a star football player from Los Angeles who did a lot of pre-game promos for the Super Bowl. Anyway, he heard me say his name, so he came back and let Mom take a picture of us together. I thought it was cool to meet him.

The game started at about 5:30 p.m. If you're a football fan at all, you know that, before the game, they have a lot of activities for the fans. One of them was passing the ball to different people all throughout the crowd, and then one person gets to be last and run out onto the field with the ball. And that lucky guy was Bunchie!

One of the less positive things I remember about sitting in the stands at the game is that I had to use all of my willpower and strength literally not to punch the girl to my right. (Of course, I would never hit a girl; Dad says *never* do that. But I wanted to.)

First of all, she wasn't even a 49ers fan or whatever. Let me back up. Normally when you go to a Chiefs game, you're with other

Chiefs fans and you're cheering together. But this girl was a Las Vegas Raiders fan, and she kept cheering for them, which was incredibly annoying. Because they weren't even there. What was that about?

Anyway, she was sitting next to Mom, then there's me, and we're Chiefs fans. Then next to me on my left was another mom and son, where the son was a Chiefs fan and his mom was a 49ers fan. He would cheer for the 49ers because his mom like them. My mom and I were cheering for the Chiefs, and this weird girl didn't like either one of them. It was all very confusing. Not at all what you expect a Super Bowl crowd to be.

The game was like a normal game, but with big jumbotron TV screens showing the play on the field, the audience, the coaches on the sidelines, whatever. Very active and lots of confusion. Then there's the live Super Bowl halftime show—which that year was Shakira and Jennifer Lopez. That made sense because they're Latina, and we were in Miami, which has a lot of people from South America, the Caribbean, and Latin countries living there. I don't know if either of them lives in Miami or if they were just visiting.

They had bracelets on the seats for everybody to wear, and when the show started, your bracelet would glow a different color depending on where you were sitting. So, everybody got to participate by waving to different parts of the music. It was a pretty good show.

More than halfway through the fourth quarter, the 49ers were ahead 20–10, and Mom thought that we should leave because I was getting tired. Later, I teased her that she wanted to leave because our team was losing. But I must admit, it had been a pretty long day by then, and I was a little tired.

You've got to understand what a sacrifice this was for her. In this world, there are football fans, and then there are *football fans!* My mom is one of those superfans who watches every minute of every game. She will even watch every minute of the drafts. But like she always says, when you learn to deal with cancer, you learn to deal with the fact that everything shifts. You've got to adapt, and in the long run, it'll all work out. So, she shrugged and said it was a good way to beat the crowd. I told you, my family likes to go early and leave early.

Mark had the limo waiting for us right outside the stadium. As we were walking out, we could hear the crowd, and the gigantic roar made you feel like the world had just exploded or something. When we got to the car, the driver was watching the game on his phone, and he showed it to us as we got in. Kansas City had just scored!

Mom then turned on her phone so she could hear her favorite hometown announcer, Mitch Holthus. For the next few minutes, between his phone and her phone, it was like we'd never left our seats. Unbelievably, in the last minutes of the game, the 49ers were at the 50-yard line when the Chiefs got the ball! With less than two minutes left, Patrick Mahomes led a SECOND touchdown drive. 31–20 Kansas City. After being 10 points down in the fourth quarter, they won their first Super Bowl in fifty years. And we were right there!

The day after the Super Bowl, we went to Mark's house, where I got to thank him in person and be a guest on his podcast. I really enjoyed it and said that I would like to do a podcast of my own, where I could interview people about how they inspire people to stay positive like he does. He really took that to heart, and because of his generosity and sponsorship, he introduced me to guys who run The Podcast Factory. That led to getting my own podcast, *Nick the Brave: Chemo, Kitties, and Canines*. (I'll tell you all about it in chapter 9 [page 99].)

The last leg of the trip was also incredible. After everything else, Mark sent us to Disney World, and we got to stay in the Animal Kingdom.

Finally, after all that fun and excitement, I was pretty tired and ready to go home. We slowly got ourselves onto the plane at about 10 in the morning. Instead of taking off right away like normal, we sat there, and sat there, and sat there until finally they announced that because of tornadoes in Nashville, the flight was cancelled. We got off the plane and found out that the next flight to Kansas City was nine hours later. It was going to be a long day and part of the night in the airport. About that time, Mom got a call from Mark's assistant who had been watching the airline schedule on her office computer. She asked what we needed, then booked us a hotel and a flight for early the next morning.

That night, I was wiped out. The hotel had two big beds, one for me and one for Mom. Just as I was about to fall asleep, I could feel it happening. The chemo had taken hold, and my hair was coming out in big clumps on the pillow.

I turned to show Mom a handful of hair and said, "Look at this."

She said, "Oh no, here we go again."

That's when I decided to take charge.

I said to her, "Cut it off. Let's just cut all my hair off right now."

After convincing her that I really meant it, she got up and got dressed, went down to the front desk, and came back with a pair of scissors and a disposable razor. She didn't get it all off, but she got enough to stop the clumping. This time I was going bald my way. And the next day when we got home, Dad gave me a proper shaved head. On my terms.

Me in the football days.

P.S. I'll tell you a secret. I wasn't very good. Sure, I looked like one—a football player, that is—but I really didn't know how to play. I didn't always know what the heck they were saying. I was too big to play running back, which is what I wanted. So, they put me on the line, where I was a guard.

Chapter 8
Here We Go Again

In 2019, after almost four years of going in and out of the hospital and clinics, from different rounds of chemo and radiation, the feeding tube, to losing my hair, and all the rest of it, I started feeling like I needed a break. Dr. Ginn thought so too, so he changed my chemo from going intravenously through my port to pills. It was like a miracle. The pills let me feel so much better.

There were about seven pills I had to take every day—really big ones and you couldn't chew them either—but I didn't mind. The difference between chemo in the port and oral chemo is not like a right-away feeling. I still felt like I was going to throw up, but it just took longer. But besides not knocking me out like the chemo and radiation together did, I was able to be up and awake more. Also, the new chemo was only five days a month, and not doing it every day meant I'd only feel really bad some days. Pretty soon, it was almost November 2019. My hair was coming back in, and I liked that. Plus, there was the added benefit that we didn't have to drive into Kansas City and back every single day. I don't mind riding in the car, but that really got to be time consuming for me and Mom.

Me with my oral chemo pills. The protocol
for using them is super strict, and you
have to be very careful with them.

What I've Learned

The steps you have to take for any medical
treatment to work right is called the *protocol*. In
this case, other people can never touch your oral
chemo pills without gloves because it can go into
their bodies through their skin.

By the end of December 2019, I was feeling better. But the MRIs
were showing that while the tumors weren't getting any bigger when
I took the pills, they weren't going away either. So, Dr. Ginn suggested we might try something called a research trial. (Remember
that in the last chapter, I mentioned going into my first trial, just
before Super Bowl LIV.)

Each trial has its own qualifications—and either you fit, or you don't. Most of the time, I didn't. But when they say you're "trying out" for a trial, it's nothing like trying out for a football team. If you don't get picked for a trial, that has nothing to do with anything you've done—right or wrong. It just means that the researchers for that one trial are looking for something different to test.

Try to remember that some of these trial drugs won't say, "Hey, I like you." It's an experiment after all! How the new drugs work with you or not can give the doctors and scientists a lot of important information either way. So, if it doesn't work, they can then try something else that maybe will work. In science, they have to test things over and over to be sure they know as much as they can about it.

Your doctor may not say all that at first. That's because you can't tell people what the drug should be doing, or they might think something's really happening when it isn't. Doctors don't want to talk you into anything. They want to know the real truth about what it does and doesn't do for you. It's really amazing how your brain works. How you can make yourself feel something or not just by the way you think about it. Your mind and your attitude are the most powerful tools you've got in this fight.

The main point of a trial like this is to help other kids who are coming behind you. And if it helps you too, that's great. Kind of like this book, I hope.

Things went along pretty well for a while, but then I started feeling worse, so I decided it would be a good time to just take a break from all of it! To go off all of the chemo completely for a while. I decided it. Not Mom or Dad, they left it up to me. At first, I didn't know what to do, but I did know that I didn't want to feel bad for a while. Dr. Ginn and I talked about it a lot, and he said we could give it a try and watch things.

Then, in November 2020, the cancer came back. Dr. Ginn put me on some new medication while he checked out other chances for me to try out for a new trial. I didn't qualify for one because my tumor wasn't big enough. I know that sounds weird, but, like I said, each group is looking for certain things in their trial, and that time they wanted tumors bigger than mine. He went on looking for more and then found another one that had to have the chemo go through an IV instead of pills, and that meant getting a new port.

Me and Mom before getting my third port installed,
just in case I make the new trial. I wanted her
to stop taking pictures, and this was the best
way to just let her have one last "good one."

This picture was taken in the special room they put you in after you've had sedation. You're supposed to relax, but I was a little nervous because I was going to get stuck. I didn't have my port in yet—I hated getting the needle again. But that time, the technician was amazing. Boom! Just like that, she was right in. I really appreciated her talent. They must have taken a gallon of blood that day. It was just gushing. Much more than before, because this trial was different, and the application tests were different too. This time they were also going to take a bone scan test (which is where they put radioactive liquid in your vein and you go into another machine for more pictures), then surgery to put in the port, and then we could finally go home.

What I've Learned
Most of your blood contains red cells (that help move oxygen in and carbon dioxide out of your body) and white cells (that fight infections). But there are also these little, colorless cell pieces called *platelets* that help your blood clot when you have an injury like a cut or bruise.

That stuff about the platelets is pretty complicated, and I don't know all about it. I do know that not having enough can be dangerous and the researchers didn't want to take any risks. Also, it had to do with my age, I think. Because I'm still growing, the places at the end of my bones can be affected harder by the chemo. That's where lots of the platelets are, and it can cause more trouble if you don't have enough.

What I've Learned
When you're growing, that actually happens at the end of your bones. For many of us, that can be where we're most sensitive to all the chemo.

Not too long after that, I learned I didn't qualify for that trial either because I didn't have enough platelets in my blood. They were looking for 100,000 platelets per a small amount of blood, and I only had 99,000! That was really rotten, because I was so close. So, we decided to wait a week to let me rest and try to build up more platelets. But then in the next test, they actually went down. If your platelets get too low, you have to have a transfusion. And that happened to me once before. We didn't want to have it happen again.

In the meantime, Dr. Ginn had a different kind of chemo for me. Might as well use that new port they put in, right? And he also said that if I could handle the first drugs, they could always add more in through my port. Seeing as how it was almost Christmas, he said I should go home, relax, and have some fun. That made a lot of sense to me too.

David, still looking out for me.

Chapter 9
Living Now and for the Future

As I've said, our family likes to travel. Quick trips, long trips, and lately because of COVID-19, lots of little trips around Kansas to visit family. We like going to Uncle Mark and Aunt Marillyn's lake house whenever we can; sometimes my cousins Kacie, Garrett, and Paige are there too. It's a pretty big lake, like one hundred yards across, but not too deep, and seven feet at the dock. It's always fun to go there, but it's also smelly—like dead fish, which is what I guess most lakes smell like.

Not too long ago, I went to Tulsa, Oklahoma, to visit my cousin Paul, who's my uncle David's son. Tulsa is about a four-hour drive from Lawrence, and you go right through the western part of the Cherokee Nation, which was cool to see.

Paul's older than me (in his thirties), and he just got married to Mackenzie. They took me camping for the first time, and we slept in tents and went rafting, along with Wes, another friend of theirs. I found a special rock, with different layers showing different times from thousands of years ago. It could even be petrified wood. (That's when a tree died millions of years ago and got buried and turned into rock.) That night, we roasted wieners on the campfire and made S'mores. The trip was good for my parents and my brother too because they got to relax at home.

Our next family trip will be to Colorado to see my cousin Ann, who's my uncle David's daughter. Ann works as an *insight strategist*, and we both have the same birthday, June 23. Different years, of course. Uncle David lives closer to us, so we get to see him a lot more. When we go there, we mainly watch football and play pool because he has a pool table. He likes taking me down to The New Dime Store in Brookside and buying me stuff. I like it too!

What I've Learned

An insight strategist is somebody who studies information a company collects about what it does and then plans how to work better. Sounds like a lot of math to me.

Earlier in 2019, before COVID-19, we went to New York. I love New York City, especially when I see a place on TV where I've been. I love that it's a big city, with big stores. Everything is big there. Thousands of people in the streets. I guess I'm just a guy who likes the action. And you can get a hot dog every day, anywhere you go, whenever you want it. In fact, I would say that the only thing I don't like about New York is that it's kind of dirty and it stinks. But I guess when you live there, you get used to it.

First, we went to the LEGO store and a place called Economy Candy that has every kind of candy you can imagine. It's just packed with candy from floor to ceiling. I told you I like candy sometimes, but most of the time I can take it or leave it. Later, we went to an M&M factory and to FAO Schwarz, the giant toy store. I'm a little too big now for that sort of stuff.

For the rest of the trip, we went to Broadway, just before they had to shut down due to the virus and saw *Beetlejuice*, *Waitress*, *Harry Potter*, and *To Kill a Mockingbird*. *Harry Potter* was three hours long, and honestly, I liked the movies better. My favorite was *To Kill a Mockingbird*, and I finally got the point of that story when Mom and I watched the movie of it before. I got right away that Tom, who was the defendant, couldn't have been guilty because the woman he was supposed to have hurt was hit by a left-handed person and Tom couldn't even use his left arm. People still blamed him anyway for something he didn't do just because of his skin color. That's ridiculous! Uncle David is a lawyer, and I told him I thought lawyers were fine, but I just don't want to be one.

We were on the seventeenth floor of the hotel when
the lights went out! Good thing they came back on.

Earlier, I told you about the Big Slick, the fundraiser in Kansas City we found three years ago when I was just going through the first chemo and radiation. That's where we met Kerri Sitrin and her husband, Henry, who live in Philadelphia. After the Big Slick, they stayed friends with our family, and she invited us to spend a weekend at their house where she had planned all this stuff for us to do.

Me and Kerri rooting for the
home team in Kansas City.

At the Big Slick, we went to the Royals game; so, in Philadelphia, we had to go to a Phillies game, right? That only seems fair. We even got to go out on the field and talk to the players.

Even though I'm really a Royals fan, I thought it
was polite to wear a Phillies shirt because all the
guys on the Phillies team were so nice to me.

When we got to Kerri's house, a friend of hers was there. She is a famous pastry chef, Monica Glass ("Chef Moni"), who taught me how to make French macarons. And they are pretty tricky to get just right. Baking's like that. In cooking, when things go wrong, you still have a chance to fix it.

What I've Learned

Everybody thinks macarons are a French cookie because that's where you see them all the time–in French cookbooks and pictures from France–but they were really invented in Italy.

Later that night, Kerri had set up dinner at a fancy restaurant called the Spice Finch. It's owned by Executive Chef Jennifer Carroll, who's been on the TV show *Top Chef* more than once. I've seen tapes of her seasons. After dinner, I got to go back into the kitchen and bother the chefs.

Me and Chef Jen in a real chef's
apron in a real restaurant.

I've been lucky enough to have had some great things happen to me on these trips and special events because my mom is always in the search for those things. That's just her. I told you we like to travel, and Mom always says she wants me to have new experiences. But even if you don't want to travel or go to big events, you can still keep busy with plenty of other stuff that you have around your house or neighborhood that keep you interested. I made a list of some of them, but whatever you decide to do, remember to go at your own pace.

Pace Yourself

There's a park behind our neighborhood. One of my friends is a girl, and she has a boyfriend. Sometimes we all walk up there to meet and talk. Those are some of my favorite times, but in the summer, when it's hot, it's hard for me to keep up. Sometimes. It bothers me when I slow them down, but they say they don't mind going at my pace. It stills wears me out for the next day, and I have to sleep in late. I'm not a late-as-noon person, but I do sleep in after a busy day.

While you have cancer, it's probably going to be like that. Personally, I hated it at first, and it used to make me frustrated and mad when I couldn't do the things I used to do, like ride my bike with the kids. Cancer does that. It just does. And some things will always be like that, there just isn't a choice. I think it's better if you just live with it! That's all!

Like football. I played for two years, and it was a lot of fun. Even if the cancer goes away completely, I won't ever be able to play again—it's just too risky after having brain tumors. But I can always be a superfan.

Ol' #20, me and the guys.

Look at What's Happening Now

So, here are some of my ideas about how to enjoy things now and still plan for the future. You're welcome to use any you want.

Be proud of what you're known for—what makes you be you.

A kid I know, Matteo Lambert, is known for running marathons to raise money for cancer. I'm known for collecting rubber arm bands. Once, I went back to Children's Mercy for some more tests, and I hadn't been to this part of the hospital for more than a year. Most of the nurses were still the same as before, and one of them said to me, "We've missed seeing you and the bands on your arms— that's how we know it's the real Nicholas."

Actually, I got the first one the year before I got cancer. My brother's troop leader gave me one that says, "No One Fights Alone." He had throat cancer, and later it seemed right for me too.

I don't go anywhere without my
bands. Even in the shower.

I've made a list of my bands from top to bottom:

- ○ The top band came from a guy named Brian Butler, and it's a bunch of different colored beads that show every shade of human skin. That is so cool to me. People can put their hand next to it and find their bead.
- ○ There's one for the Philadelphia Phillies that I got on that trip Kerri set up.
- ○ There's one for the University of Kansas Jayhawks.
- ○ Then there's a little black one with a spiritual saying.
- ○ Next is the "No One Fights Alone" I told you about.
- ○ There's one from Baby Jay's Legacy of Hope. That's a charity that was started by parents who lost their daughter to cancer.

- I've got a band from the trip to Sporting KC, the professional soccer team.
- There's one from the pirate shop at the Kansas City Renaissance Fair. (You saw a picture of the pirates in chapter 2, page 20).
- There's a black band from my friend Mark Evans. He calls himself The Dealmaker.
- There's a band from Alex's Lemonade Stand, which raises money for cancer research.
- Finally, the last one is from Toys for Toys.

Knowing who you are also means accepting which things that you'd like to change. Take me, for example. I am a worrier. Like I hate it when my dogs get out. What if something happens to them? What if they get hit by a car or something? I couldn't stand that! My family calls it "circling" because I kind of get into a loop where I worry about something then decide it will be okay, then go back to worrying about it again. I talked to a psychologist about it once, but she didn't think much of it.

Ask for a pet to take care of.

My family teases and calls me the "animal hoarder." My favorites are dogs and cats, but what kind of pet you get depends on what you like or if anybody in your family has allergies. Having pets is a big responsibility. My dogs play rough, and while they don't mean any hurt or anything, they sometimes bite each other. Those places can turn into these masses, and you might have to take them to the vet. Animals get cancer too, but we don't think that's what they are. Just something to keep an eye on. Our dog Jingle had surgery on her ears and had to wear a cone. That wasn't cancer either.

We have six animals in the house now. My poor mom has to get rid of fur and hair everywhere, constantly! I told you their names before: Briar, the wire-haired terrier; Jingle, a black Lab; Loki, a choco-late Lab; and then Rosy, the blonde Lab. Rosy was my Christmas pres-ent in 2016, and she's the calmest. She doesn't like conflict.

What I've Learned

Lab is short for Labrador Retriever. A lot of people think they're hunting dogs from England, but they're really from Newfoundland, an island off of Canada, even though it's right next to a part of the mainland that's called Labrador. That seems weird. Most of all, I like the name of the island-New-found-land. Get it?

Finally, we've got the cats, Sweet'ems and Mr. Fox. Sometimes we even babysit dogs and cats for family when they go on vacation. My mom says we've got so many, one more's not going to make a differ-ence. I've also had a bird and hamsters. And I'd like to get another bird one day, but right now Mom says, "No, way."

David, Me, and Dad. You can see that with all the critters in our house we have to have tons of Christmas stockings.

Learn something new to expand your mind.

I like painting, cooking crab, and baking, but that's easy stuff I've always wanted to do. I think it's important to pick new things you've never tried before. Like, a lot of new people are moving to Kansas from Mexico, Central America, and South America. So, I'm also trying to learn Spanish now. That way, when I'm a doctor and Spanish-speaking people come into the hospital, I'll be able to understand them and them me.

Maybe the biggest new thing I've tried is doing my podcasts.

Doing My Podcast

One of the people we met at the Big Slick fundraiser for Children's Mercy was Nick Paradise and his wife, Maddie. I told you about him before. They're both entrepreneurs. Nick recycles plastics into beach furniture and picnic tables. Maddie has a company that makes earbuds. Well, anyway, Nick is the guy who introduced us to Mark Evans. I've also talked about Mark before because he's the one who sent me to Super Bowl LIV and gave me the black band I wear.

Since meeting at the Super Bowl, we've kept in touch and follow each other on Instagram. Mark also gave me a whole set of equipment and introduced me to people at The Podcast Factory, who have helped me set up my own podcast where I interview people about how they stay positive and inspire others to stay positive. Some of the key questions I ask are: "What's the biggest accomplishment you've had in your life, and how did you do it? What's the biggest impact you've had on other people's lives?"

The name of my podcast is *Nick the Brave: Chemo, Kitties, and Canines*. Listen to it wherever podcasts are available: Apple Podcasts, Audible, Spotify, the Podcast Factory, and more. (I'll tell you how I came up with Chemo, Kitties, and Canines a little later.)

I've been lucky enough to interview some pretty interesting and successful people. Just a few of them are:

- Wendi McLendon-Covey, who plays the mom on the TV show, *The Goldbergs*.

- Father Mick.

- Darcy Krause, my former elementary school principal.

- Brian Hanni, the voice of the University of Kansas Jayhawks.

- Chef Jay Juan, a private chef for some of the Kansas City Chiefs. His favorite food is also crab! He's gonna teach me some secrets about preparing it after COVID-19.

- Dana Powell, who plays Pameron Tucker, the sister of Eric Stonestreet's character on *Modern Family*. They also call her Pam N' Cheese and Pamburger, which I think is funny.

- Valorie Burton, who is a life coach, author, motivational speaker, and entrepreneur. She is the founder of the Coaching and Positive Psychology Institute.

- Mike Griswald, a retired Army colonel and a former city mayor. He taught me stuff about leadership.

- Bob Fescoe, the announcer for Sports Radio 610 in Kansas City.

- Matteo Lambert, the kid who likes to run marathons. He got this idea to run them to raise money for and in honor of kids who are fighting cancer. And he ran one for me. He puts your name and picture on a cape and runs with it. He says it gives him superpowers. He won't take it off and keeps going.

I've interviewed lots of other people (over sixty in all), including a hip-hop professor and other kids with cancer. One was a kid named

Ian, who's about eleven years old. I met him in a roundabout way, which happens often when you reach out to a lot of people. My mom has a friend and colleague named Ken Williams (who also did a podcast with me)—and he knew a graphic designer who is Ian's sister.

Ian was lucky with his cancer because they could take it out. He says he's very shy—not like my personality. And when we talked over Zoom, he was in the hospital for more chemo. I sent him some LEGOs, and he appreciated that. I told him I'd be his friend.

The only qualification for being on my podcast is that you've got to be a positive person. I only interview people who are positive. The person I'd most like to interview would be Dwayne "The Rock" Johnson.

Mark and I are also talking about doing a YouTube channel. My idea is to go on and say something like, "Hey, I'm Nicholas, blah blah blah, I've got cancer, and I'd like to answer any of your questions if you just learned you've got it or hear about your experiences." I would be setting up a back-and-forth thing. This will be another way to help kids stay positive.

Future Plans

Most of all, you want to keep making plans for the future.

My main goal is to study medicine. I'm definitely interested in medicine and science, because having cancer has taught me how to understand what kids go through. I understand it. And at the University of Kansas, they even have scholarships available for kids like us who have had cancer. I'm sure that's true at other schools too.

I'm not a certified speaker, but my mom set me up to do a motivational speech for the teachers at Eisenhower Elementary in Fort Leavenworth, Kansas. I think I could really enjoy doing that because I like people. Somebody told me once that I could make friends with a stop sign. That's why when COVID-19 is over, I'd like to go places and give speeches to big groups of people.

Like I mentioned earlier, someday I want to start this organization called Chemo, Kitties, and Canines. The point of it is to connect kids who have cancer with animal shelters and groups trying to get cats and dogs into good homes. The idea came to me one day when we were riding in the car, going to the hospital. Wouldn't it be great if we set up something where kids who are getting chemo could adopt a dog or cat that needed a home? And then the name Chemo, Kitties, and Canines, or CKC for short, just came into my mind. It seemed perfect. I thought I could help not only other kids getting treatment, but I could also help the animals in shelters. It's something that would work anywhere. My mom has a friend who has a friend who owns a rescue farm, where she gives food and shelter to animals that need forever homes. It's the coolest place, with dogs and cats just roaming around her farm. This CKC is an idea that any kid can start in his or her own hometown.

If I had a million Make-A-Wishes—they would all be just more of what I did before COVID-19: going on trips, being with my friends more, just hanging out with my family.

Me, looking forward to the New Year, 2021!

P.S. Just passed my driver's learner permit class. We start early in Kansas because so many kids already drive the farm equipment.

Afterword

By Geri Parscale

Almost twenty years ago as a school administrator in Leavenworth, Kansas, I'd followed the work of Richard and Rebecca DuFour, principal authors and consultants with Solution Tree, a company providing professional development for educators. And the publishers of *What I Wish I Knew Before Cancer*. But on this first encounter, I wrote to them saying how much my staff and I had benefited from their authors. They replied by asking if I would consider telling my story at a conference. Some years later, I'd just been asked to work with them as a presenter myself—when I became pregnant with Nicholas.

Ten years after that, Nicholas was diagnosed with cancer. It was July, which in the educational development world is like our preparation for the Super Bowl. August is when educators have the *time* for professional development, and we are really geared up for work. My schedule had easily over twenty presentation days, including travel and preparation time. We were extremely busy. I called them and their first response was don't worry about anything. Take all the time you need. We'll get people to handle your schedule.

A few months after that, I was back presenting again, and that particular week I was in a school in Midland, Texas. I'd tried to get home to Kansas for the weekend but had gotten stuck there because of storms. Sitting in that hotel room, and what seemed to be out of the blue, I got an email from Jeff Jones, the CEO of Solution Tree, asking if I'd set up a GoFundMe account. I was touched that he'd thought to connect with me, but I thought, "No way, I can't ask people for money. Where I'm from, you don't do that." But Jeff's suggestion spurred me to explore that avenue, and later, I did set up an account to help with the expenses of Nicholas's care.

At every point, around every corner of this journey, Solution Tree has been there for me. Often before I even knew that I needed help.

Of course, as the parent of a child with cancer, you will often hear, "You are living every parent's worst nightmare. What do you need? How can we help?" People everywhere *want* to help; they just don't know what to do or how to go about it. They're afraid. Afraid of saying the wrong thing. Afraid of then not knowing what to say when you respond. Mostly they know that they can't give you what you really need—for your child not to have cancer. And so, for all of those complicated and heartfelt reasons, people often don't say anything.

I've learned that it's important to be mindful of the importance of communication. Communicating ideas, hopes, fears, and needs with your family, your neighbors, your friends, your work colleagues, and certainly with the doctors, nurses, and therapists who are guiding you through the long road of your child's cancer. Just trying to help them understand that they don't have to walk on eggshells when around you. I often tell people that I appreciate when you *just ask me*, because then I can tell you.

There are many support partners in this process. We are partners as a family; we are partnering with the medical team and organizations supporting families with cancer. And Solution Tree has been an important partner for us throughout this—allowing me to take time off when needed, being there with an assignment when I needed to keep my mind busy with something other than my own heartache.

If you're reading this story and want to help a family experiencing cancer—just do. Pick up the phone, and say something like, "Tomorrow, I'm making a big pot of soup for my family; may I bring some over for yours? I won't stay; I'm just dropping it off for you to eat now or put in your freezer."

Then just do it. You don't have to say anything else. There is not a family out there going through this who will turn you down. And I promise you that when that family closes the door after your visit, they will experience a healing moment. A quiet gratitude and peace because someone cared.

If you're reading this and your child has cancer, perhaps just beginning the process, you already know all about the heartache and frustration. You already know that this isn't going to be easy. But what I also want to convey is that there are partners everywhere out there who are eager and willing to help. My humble advice is to stick to your routines, keep your life as orderly as you can, communicate with everyone, and most importantly, accept help when it's given. As Father Mick often tells me, "Just lean in."

About Getting Through the Day

Everyone has their own strategy for living as normally as you can on a daily basis. Maybe you have other children, or a job with all of its pressures and responsibilities. My work has often been a godsend because it gives me something to focus on outside of our family situation. Of course, Nicholas and his cancer are *never* out of my thoughts, but living with cancer is a marathon, and there are many days and hours when being occupied with others helps you keep yourself on track. If you don't have a job opportunity, you might consider community or church work for a few hours a week. In any case, you sometimes have to remind yourself to breathe and hug the people you love.

With that said, I am also the kind of individual who finds that staying very organized gives me some control when so very much else in life is simply in the hands of others. God, certainly, but also the medical professionals who monitor Nicholas's health. Even the scientists who are desperately trying to find a cure for cancer, all of these positive forces that can help my child, are beyond my abilities as a parent. I'm helpless.

And because I have so many things in my life that are outside of my control right now, it is a comfort to me to meticulously plan my days.

This is certainly one of the things I've read which can help combat depression and anxiety: that if you get up each morning and you know that you have this, this, and this to get done at these certain times—either you have a meeting, or a chemo appointment, or the laundry—anything that has to be accomplished—then having a structure can keep you going. I can only speak for myself, but staying organized keeps me in a better frame of mind. That's why I have a day journal and a duplicate paper calendar because, God forbid, I take the chance of only having everything on my computer and cell phone. I have lists and notes everywhere to keep me on track.

My favorite calendar has large blank spaces for each part of the day, so I can keep the phone numbers I need to call and the names of people I need to remember. All of those individuals who are partners in Nicholas's life. Because fighting cancer is a community experience.

So, in late October of 2020, when we had reached the point in Nicholas's treatment where the chemo was just slowing down but not eradicating his cancer, we were offered the chance for a new experimental drug through a cancer trial. I was set. I had all the necessary steps perfectly organized.

November was a fresh new month with lots of blank spaces on my calendar. I'll share some of the entries with you now.

November 2, 2020
One lesion increased in size by a few millimeters in each direction, and the other measurable tumor is essentially the same. Dr. Ginn said there's better visualization of possible new tumors throughout the brain and spine, and all these areas hint at possible progression. But it's complicated by a change in their MRI protocols during the past month. In other words, we may be seeing them now because the new MRIs are clearer.

Dr. G was happy they hadn't increased that much in size, but he cautioned us because as time passes, they will continue to enlarge.

November 3, 2020
When I asked Nicholas if he wanted to go back to chemo again, there was no hesitation. He does; so that's what we'll do. No more pills. The IV will begin on November 9 and last for 21 days.

November 4, 2020
So, here's what I know. Tomorrow, we will arrive at hospital at 8 a.m. He has to have EKG with this study as well as blood work. Then, will have surgery to replace the port at 11:00 a.m. Then a new step that's unique to this study because of his age—bone scans to check growth plates. So that will be done after the surgery. It will be a long day for sure.

The next morning, we went into the hospital, and I was in good spirits. Nicholas had just been given his pre-op sedation before the reinsertion of the port for the chemotherapy trial. I was taking a video and then a selfie of the two of us.

Nicholas was so funny. He kept saying, "Stop filming everything!"

He was really tired that morning. I asked what was wrong, and he said emphatically, "Nothing's wrong!"

But I knew different. Yes, I thought, he's a typical teenager. Or he's becoming haunted by all of this. It's finally catching up to him. Bothering him. This day it was more like frustration. As if he were saying in his mood and actions, "Why can't I get this new therapy right now? Why is this taking so long? Why can't we just do it?"

And those were answers I couldn't give.

This could be it. The trial that will finally kick it.

November 5, 2020, Afternoon
Okay a glitch in plans. He didn't make it. His platelets are at 99,000. To qualify for study, they need to be at 100,000. So, he does not qualify. Still going to get port and see what else we can do in coming weeks.

That day was so deflating I can't even put it into words. I held up as well as could be expected, but even though I tried so hard, there were a few tears. And for the first time ever, Nicholas got upset because I was upset. He told me that he didn't like it when I cried. That was a sobering reality for me. I'd thought I was pretty much controlling myself in front of him. When I'd cried a little bit before, it didn't seem to bother him. During those times, *he* had actually comforted me. This was something new.

November 6, 2020
So good news!!!

They are going to retest him next Thursday for an increase in his platelet count. He was at 99,000, and it needed to be 100,000, so we're really hoping that one thousand can be made up this week. I added all the chemo appointments into my calendars. Not really a lot we can do to help the platelets increase except for rest etc. which he's more than happy to do!

November 12, 2020
His platelet levels went down. 93,000 per 100,000. So, he didn't make it. It was lower. He was rejected for another trial.

That's when I ripped all of the November pages out of my journals. I just lost it. But the very next morning, Friday, November 13, I woke up and started a new calendar.

And then God blessed me.

First, Dr. Ginn called to say that he'd just learned of a brand-new trial that was being organized at St. Jude in Memphis. *The* St. Jude. One of world's premier children's cancer research hospitals.

And then He blessed me again because I got an email from my contact at Solution Tree. There'd been a scheduling emergency with one of the presenters, and if I were available, they needed me the week of December 16–20—for a virtual workshop for a school outside of Washington, DC, that I've worked with for years—then another virtual conference with a school in West Virginia that I've also worked with forever. Next, I was to drive to Oklahoma City where I had virtual conferences first for a school in Wyoming, then Florida, then back to the school in Washington, DC. The following morning there was an in-person appointment in Oklahoma City. Finally, the day after that, I was to be back in Kansas City for another in-person workshop. Of course, there was the financial blessing, but then I thought, "Now I can make it until Thanksgiving with a whole new list of things that have to get done."

I felt that maybe this was God's way of saying, "Hold up. Take a breath."

There have been some very large bolts from God in all of this, and I know that Solution Tree has been one of them. Once during the very first round of chemotherapy, Nicholas was very, very sick. He'd lost a tremendous amount of weight. I hated leaving him and so they said I should bring him with me to an important training session in their Bloomington, Indiana, home office, which is just south of Indianapolis.

I couldn't believe it. Jeff and others at Solution Tree had set up an incredible weekend for Nicholas. He got to meet members of the Indiana University football team. They talked, joked around, and tossed balls back and forth. One of the players even took off his glove and gave it to Nicholas.

November 24, 2020
He did not make the trial at Saint Jude. Not enough "positive markers." Whatever that means. I'm not sure. Dr. G will be working on other options. Probably the treatment that was the backbone of the original study at Children's Mercy, but not in any official trial.

Here is the odd thing—during that pivotal month of November 2020—as I would pray, I would have to stop and ask God what to pray for. I had never been sure that St. Jude was the right direction in the first place. But, you know, they say St. Jude's the best. Like any parents, we would have done anything to get our child the best. And although Nicholas would've done whatever Dr. Ginn said to do, he *really, really* didn't want to leave the team we have here. So, I'm convinced that God has shown us the right path.

January 11, 2021
Nicholas had a horrible weekend. Horrible
headaches and pain in his back. He can't keep
anything down. Dr. Ginn got us into Children's for
an MRI tomorrow afternoon.

January 12, 2021, 3 p.m.
They're concerned that he will throw up on the
MRI table. So, Dr. G ordered a CT scan and then
having us go to emergency to wait. May be
admitted based on results.

8:35 p.m.
Going to admit. Will know more tomorrow.

January 13, 2021, 7 a.m.
The initial CT scan did not show any huge
blockages in the brain, and that's a good thing.
The plan today is to run an MRI and get a more
complete picture. After that, I am not sure. Dave
stayed the night with him as I have two schools
that I'm working with today. Will know more
this afternoon.

Nicholas has never said, "Why Me?" He's *never ever* been in that frame of mind. He's always been the most positive of all of us—always just moving forward to get to whatever had to be done to beat cancer. Eager to learn and explore. He's enjoyed putting together this book and sincerely wants others to learn from what he's been through.

Now with the medicine to keep him out of pain, he's happy to be home. With the four of us—our own immediate family. With his aunts and uncles and cousins when possible. With his pets. To play virtual video games with Treavor. To see his other friends and laugh.

About the ending—the only time we spoke of it, I planned on how to bring it up at just the right time. Casually. Part of another conversation. And Nicholas was, well, he was just Nicholas. His regular, casual self.

As if tossing it off and moving on to do something more important, he said, "I'm worried about that too sometimes. Not all the time. Not today."

So, for now, we have today.

Appendix A
Dr. Ginn's Notes

Nicholas was ten years old in July 2016, when he presented to Lawrence Memorial Hospital in Lawrence, Kansas, with nausea, vomiting, and headache. A CT of his head was ordered, revealing a pineal area brain tumor with hydrocephalus (high pressure) on his brain. He was transferred to Children's Mercy Hospital in Kansas City, Missouri, where an MRI revealed he also had local spread of tumor along the tentorium intracranially and spinal leptomeningeal enhancement consistent with distant metastasis. He underwent biopsy of his tumor on 7/10/16, and pathology revealed a Grade IV (WHO Classification) pineoblastoma.

Nicholas started chemotherapy as per ACNS0332 Regimen B and received daily carboplatin and weekly vincristine with radiation treatments on Monday–Friday. His last radiation treatment and carboplatin infusion was completed on 9/20/16. He was admitted for cycle 1 chemo on 11/1/16. Vincristine was held since starting maintenance chemo due to peripheral motor neuropathy. He completed six planned cycles of maintenance chemotherapy with the last dose of chemotherapy administered on 4/20/17. MRI on 5/7/18 at one year off therapy showed some nodular enhancing foci, concerning for recurrence of pineoblastoma, which needed to be followed closely.

Nick returned two months later, now fourteen months after completion of initial treatment, for a repeat MRI on 7/16/18 which showed several intracranial lesions and areas of possible leptomeningeal disease in the brain, confirming recurrence of his disease. He immediately began additional treatment.

Initially, Nicholas began relapse therapy following ACNS0821 on 8/6/18 and responded well to treatment with resolution of metastatic sites; however, he developed significant fatigue and poor quality of life, so chemotherapy was stopped after seven cycles. He was then referred for repeat radiation and was treated from 5/6/19 through 6/10/19. The treatment consisted of: 12.6 Gy/9.8 Gy to the brain in seven fractions in an irregularly shaped, very modulated field matched to his diagnostic treatments from 2016 to bring the composite brain dose (combined with prior treatment) to about 50 Gy, the periventricular tissue to 54 Gy, and initial primary area to 64 Gy. This was followed by a boost to 37.8 Gy to the metastatic lesions—four in total (left frontal, left and right temporal, and left cerebellum).

His one-month post radiation MRI on 7/15/19 showed no evidence of disease, so an MRI was scheduled for three months later. The MRI of 10/2/19 revealed further progression of disease, requiring additional therapy. At the time of this second relapse, Nick chose to participate in a clinical trial. His tumor responded well initially to the chemotherapy, but eventually progressed again, requiring removal from the clinical trial.

Nick is currently taking oral chemotherapy with a goal of keeping his tumor stable as long as possible while he focuses on maintaining the best quality of life while spending time with those he loves. He will continue to be monitored closely with MRI, and additional therapy options will be sought by his family and oncology team.

Kevin F. Ginn, M.D., Pediatric Neuro-Oncology
Director, Pediatric Brain Tumor Program Interim
Director, Experimental Therapeutics in Pediatric Oncology
Division of Hematology/Oncology/BMT Children's
Mercy Hospital and Clinics

Appendix B
My Cancer Treatment Timetable

Two important words to understand about chemotherapy treatments are *cycle* and *round*. A round is a group of times you go in for treatment. A cycle is the space between cancer treatments. So, your first round of chemo could have any number of cycles and a different number of rounds. That depends on how many different chemicals or radiation treatments are used.

These dates are as close as I can remember. Dr. Ginn keeps the real records at the hospital. My dates may not be perfect, but I want to show you how it can be like a carnival ride, like a drop tower or a roller coaster. Stop and go. Up and down. That's just all part of it.

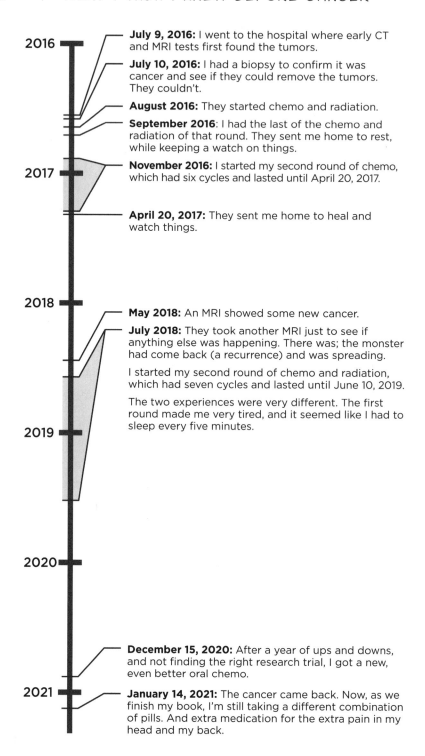

2016

July 9, 2016: I went to the hospital where early CT and MRI tests first found the tumors.

July 10, 2016: I had a biopsy to confirm it was cancer and see if they could remove the tumors. They couldn't.

August 2016: They started chemo and radiation.

September 2016: I had the last of the chemo and radiation of that round. They sent me home to rest, while keeping a watch on things.

2017

November 2016: I started my second round of chemo, which had six cycles and lasted until April 20, 2017.

April 20, 2017: They sent me home to heal and watch things.

2018

May 2018: An MRI showed some new cancer.

July 2018: They took another MRI just to see if anything else was happening. There was; the monster had come back (a recurrence) and was spreading.

I started my second round of chemo and radiation, which had seven cycles and lasted until June 10, 2019.

The two experiences were very different. The first round made me very tired, and it seemed like I had to sleep every five minutes.

2019

2020

December 15, 2020: After a year of ups and downs, and not finding the right research trial, I got a new, even better oral chemo.

2021

January 14, 2021: The cancer came back. Now, as we finish my book, I'm still taking a different combination of pills. And extra medication for the extra pain in my head and my back.